The Eyes of the Blind

The Eyes of the Blind

Alison Morgan

Oxford University Press 1986
Oxford Toronto Melbourne

Oxford University Press, Walton Street,
Oxford OX2 6DP

Oxford New York Toronto
Delhi Bombay Calcutta Madras Karachi
Petaling Jaya Singapore Hong Kong Tokyo
Nairobi Dar es Salaam Cape Town
Melbourne Auckland

and associated companies in
Beirut Berlin Ibadan Nicosia

Oxford is a trade mark of Oxford University Press

© Alison Morgan 1986
First published 1986

British Library Cataloguing in Publication Data
Morgan, Alison
The eyes of the blind.
I. Title
823'.914[J] PZ7

ISBN 0–19–271542–9

All rights reserved. No part of this publication may be reproduced, stored in a retrieval system, or transmitted, in any form or by any means, electronic, mechanical, photocopying, recording or otherwise, without the prior permission of Oxford University Press

This book is sold subject to the condition that it shall not, by way of trade or otherwise, be lent, resold, hired or otherwise circulated without the publisher's prior consent in any form of binding or cover other than that in which it is published and without a similar condition including this condition being imposed on the subsequent purchaser

Typeset in Bembo by Fontwise
Printed in Great Britain by
Biddles Ltd., Guildford

To Nicholas and Robert

PART ONE

Chapter 1

The first time I saw Adad he was cradling my dead father in his arms. Blood and tears streamed down his upturned face from his blinded eyes, and he wailed, but softly, like a sheepdog torn by wolves and left to die. I should have feared and hated him, for he wore the purple of the Assyrian monsters, but I did not. Perhaps I had already used up all the fear and hatred that can be stored in the body of a twelve-year-old boy, because for two days I had been watching the destruction of the city of Lachish.

They had come early in the morning. We had been told they were coming, but no one expected them so soon. That was the story of the Assyrian campaign. Wherever they went, they arrived before they were expected, and though they could not have been fiercer or more cruel than the reputation that ran before them, the terror of their arrival was more frightful than anything the waiting people had imagined.

I watched them approaching with the rest of the inhabitants of Lachish clustered on the inner wall, I and my father; two strangers among strangers. It was not our city. My father had been sent on business from the Temple. He was not one of the select ruling body of priests, but dealt with the administrative side, and had been put in charge of collecting the offerings from the outlying regions. I do not think he really liked the job, for he was a gentle, scholarly man who hated asking people for anything, especially when they told him sad stories of poor harvests and hungry babies. Although I did not realize it at the time, I think, on looking back, that he was probably given the task more because he was the son of the great teacher, Isaiah, than on his own merits. Knowing this, he did the work as conscientiously as he could, without complaining.

It was my mother who suggested I go with him on this trip to Lachish. 'It will be good for the boy to see a bit of the world,' she told my father, 'and Benjamin will be company for you, and big enough to be useful.' If she had known that Sennacherib's army was already hurtling down the Phoenician coast, I would never have been allowed to go, but all my life we had lived in expectation of an Assyrian invasion, and on the face of it there was no reason to believe Lachish was in any more immediate danger than Jerusalem itself.

So we had gone, and the short journey there had been one of the happiest times of my life. My father rode his old mare, and I had a donkey. A couple of Temple servants followed with two pack-animals. We followed the southern route, through Bethlehem and Hebron, because my father had business to transact in both those places. Then we turned our backs on the rising sun and followed the old road that drops gently down to Lachish a dozen miles away through valleys greener and more fertile than ever I had seen around Jerusalem. It was spring time, so there was still water in most of the brooks and the banks were golden with crown daisies. Sometimes flocks of long-legged goats and sheep streamed down to drink at a watering-place, but usually they were up on the hills, grazing among the rock roses and anemones, watched by an old man or a couple of children. The hills were as full of stones as a pomegranate, but as we approached Lachish the valley widened and we came upon fields of young corn and tangled gourd and cucumber plants, a few vineyards, and quantities of fig and olive trees.

It is hard to remind myself how peaceful Lachish appeared when we first came in sight of the city. Like Jerusalem, it sits like a hat on the crown of a hill, and is surrounded, not just by one massive wall, six metres thick, but two, one lowish down on the side of the hill, the other within and above it. Those walls, golden in the setting sun, not only startled by their beauty, but held within their embrace a promise of rest, food and safety.

They did give us all that, for a few days, but looking back, I realize that the magic of our journey ended as we passed in through the great gate, high up on the slope of the hillside. During the whole of our ride from Jerusalem, my father and I had shared not only the road together, but our hunger and tiredness, our conversations and our silences. In the past, I had built up my picture of my father from narrow glimpses, such as one gets of the countryside around Jerusalem by walking along the inner side of the great wall and peering out through the arrow-slits. Life at home was so full of other people, my ebullient mother and talkative sisters, my two noisy younger brothers, and half a dozen aunts, uncles and grandparents, some of whom lived with us, others nearby. They were all members of my mother's family, for she came from the line of Aaron, the first High Priest, from whom all the inner circle of the priesthood claim descent. My mother's father had been the official state chronicler, and his two sons, my uncles, were both important figures in the priestly hierarchy, especially Shebna, who was the Temple Treasurer.

My father's father, the famous Isaiah, did not live with us, but in a special building set apart for him in the Priestly College, except when he was out in the desert hills communing with Jehovah, our God. Sometimes he visited us, and when he did everybody fell silent, because it did not seem right to talk about ordinary things when such a celebrated holy man was in the room, but nobody liked to talk about sacred things either, because it seemed presumptuous in the presence of such an expert. Grandfather Isaiah never seemed to notice or be embarrassed by the silences, but I was.

The silence that lay between my father and me on that journey was quite different. It was like the silence that lies between the seed falling into the ground and the shoot that springs up with the first rain. Talk blossomed out of it whenever the moment was right. I had always liked my quiet father whenever I thought about him, which was not often, but on that journey I learned to love him.

Our visits to Bethlehem and Hebron did not really interfere with our enjoyment for they were small places where the visit of the Temple Steward was an event of some importance. Everything was all ready for him when we arrived and a night's lodging had been arranged, so there was little for my father to do except thank people in his pleasant way and ask after old friends. I, too, was made welcome for his sake and I began to feel for the first time that my father was something more than just Isaiah's son and my mother's husband, and that I shared in his status.

In Lachish things were very different. I had not realized what a big place it was, nor that it regarded itself as pretty important. It stands nearer the great thoroughfare between Assyria and Egypt than Jerusalem does, and all kinds of traders and diplomats pass through it. It was swarming with foreigners, most of them speaking some kind of Aramaic, or one of the Semitic dialects spoken by the common people all around us, but there were some, dark Ethiopians and pale people from across the Great Sea, who spoke utter gibberish as far as I was concerned. The citizens seemed to regard their city as quite as important as Jerusalem, and treated my father in a very offhand manner, I thought. I got quite irritated with him for taking their negligence so meekly, and it spoiled the old relationship. Not that we had much time for conversation—he was too busy trying to attend to all the business, which took a lot more time as he had to see to everything himself without any local help.

As the days passed, I began to realize that they were not only offhand; they were frightened. My father must have known this, too, and it worried him that he could not get his work completed and take me quickly back to Jerusalem. I heard one of the servants urging him to do just that. My father replied that he could not leave till he had discharged his responsibilities, but that he would like the two servants to return straight away and take me with them.

I said I did not want to go. All through the dissatisfying days in Lachish I had been looking forward to the return journey. As soon as we were out of the town, I thought, we would be back on the previous happy footing and everything would be all right again. Besides, how could I go back to my mother leaving him to face danger alone?

There was no real danger, he said; he would be quite safe. Then, I asked, why was he sending me away? He smiled then, and said he would try his best to get everything tied up by the morning, in which case we could all leave together, only I must promise that, if he did not succeed, I would set off with the servants without him.

By the morning it was too late. The servants had fled in the night, taking both pack-animals and our mounts, or someone else had found two of them unguarded and helped themselves; meanwhile, Sennacherib's army was pouring like a swarm of bees up the valley from the north. Only to the south-east, along the road to Hebron, was there any way of escape.

But there was no way of escape out of Lachish—not for my father, that is. The great gates were slammed shut and bolted, and soldiers were piling rocks and wood against them. Only the small side gate was left open, and under the eyes of the guards streamed the old, the women and the children, carrying bedding and bowls and chickens and sacks of meal—anything they could grab to carry away, to whatever safe hiding-place they could find—anywhere, anywhere away from the terror of Sennacherib's army. But no fighting men were allowed through. The guards saw to that.

My father came with me to the gate, and would have borne the shame of fleeing with the women and children for my sake, but was turned back.

'I am a Temple official,' he said. 'This is not my city,

and I have no weapon, and no skill to use one if I had. This is my child, whom I must take home to his family.'

'No weapon?' they said, and looked him up and down, sneering. 'Then use those white hands to tear up stones; or use your influence with Jehovah to turn back these marauding beasts in their tracks.'

We went up to the walls, he and I. We stood in silence for a while, watching the swarming invaders winding nearer. They looked harmless enough at that distance, except when a shaft of sunlight glinted on a lance or helmet. At the head of one column they appeared to be carrying three white forked pennants, dangling from poles.

'In a little while, you must go,' my father said at length. 'You can join the other refugees—more than likely most of them will take the road to Hebron and from there you can make your own way back to Jerusalem. I wish I knew you would find safety there—but at least you will be with the family.'

'I would rather stay here with you,' I said. Was it true? Either way, I was afraid. I did not dare say more, in case my voice betrayed my fear and I shamed myself in front of these strangers. So we were both silent.

'We have always known this would happen,' my father said finally. 'Do you know how old I am?'

'Yes,' I said, surprised at the unexpected question. 'Thirty-four.'

'That is the length of time your grandfather has been prophesying that the Assyrians are the servants of Jehovah, come to punish us for our sins. That, and longer.'

'Yes, I suppose so,' I said. It was true, I knew, but Isaiah had been prophesying for years and years, and nothing had happened, so I had stopped paying much attention.

My father went on. 'One of my memories is of being taken by the hand by my father Isaiah to meet the king—Ahaz, that is—at the Gihon spring. Ahaz was worried about the water supply for Jerusalem in the event of a seige.'

'By the Assyrians?'

'No, not by the Assyrians. By Syria and Samaria, who threatened to attack us if we didn't agree to join forces with them in a revolt against Assyria.'

'Surely we would want to do that anyway?'

'Isaiah said no. He said it was no use making any kind of alliances against Assyria because it was God's will that the Assyrians should destroy our nation—maybe then, maybe later; maybe much later. He said what mattered was not making alliances or stockpiling weapons, but putting ourselves right with God.'

'He still says that.'

'Yes. He has been saying it for more than thirty-four years.'

I remember looking up into my father's face as he stood there, quietly watching death march up to him on the walls of this city of strangers. It was calm, and sad, and somehow puzzled. I was puzzled, too, and angry. I had never seen my father cheat, or bully or betray anybody; but I had seen him pay money out of his own pocket rather than grind it out of the poor, and then drink well water and dress in plain robes, unlike the rest of the Temple staff, so that my mother would not suffer for his generosity. What had he done that God should send this army of wolves to destroy him?

'It's not fair,' I said. 'You've always obeyed the Commandments.'

'You mean God isn't fair?' asked my father. Most people would have just told me off for questioning the wisdom of God, or said I was too young to understand these things. My father took my words and turned them over in his mind, sharing the question with me. He drew patterns on the parapet with his finger, idly, as he pondered and then stared thoughtfully at his fingertip, stained now with the pale stone dust.

'This dust,' he said, 'do you think, if you gave it the choice of becoming a boy like you for a few years, it would take it?'

'Well, yes, I suppose so,' I said. 'I mean—it's got nothing to lose, has it?'

'You wouldn't think so, would you? But supposing it spent all its boy-years cursing you, who had given it these years, for not giving it more of them?'

'I'd say, I know just how you feel,' I muttered. That answer would have earned me an hour-long lecture from the old rabbi who taught me, but my father just put his arms round my shoulder.

'That's only for now,' he said. 'But nothing that happens to you or me can take away the last six days. I'm not going to wish it away by saying I should never have brought you with me. Wishing things undone, even hard things, is like wishing you had never left off being dust.' He rubbed his finger clean on his robe, and looked at his hands again.

'I shall not use my white hands for throwing stones,' he said. 'I've no aptitude for it.'

'Then why stay?' I asked. 'Why get killed for nothing?'

He turned his hands about, studying them. 'They are quite useful sort of hands,' he said. 'As soon as you have gone, I will take them to a doctor, for there must be doctors in this great city, and see if he can use them to bind up wounds and apply ointments.'

A man nearby made a sudden exclamation of disgust. 'Money!' he said. 'It will buy you anything.' He was looking down the slopes of the wall to where the refugees stumbled away from the little gate. For some reason, the flow had slowed to a trickle, and there now appeared, among the few weeping women clutching their babies, a finely dressed man on horseback, with two or three women swathed in rich cloaks, and a party of servants.

'How did he get through?' I exclaimed.

'Bribed the guards, no doubt,' said the man. 'Can't blame him. There's a fellow somewhere in this city been collecting the Temple dues, they say. Now if I could get my hands on that man, I'd be out of this city as fast as he'd be out of his body.'

I glanced quickly at my father, first in alarm, then in hope, but he showed no sign of having heard the man. He must have done, though, because when the man went on to say, 'But no doubt the Temple Steward will have bought himself a passage hours ago and be half-way to Hebron by now,' he turned and looked at him, and said mildly, 'I am sorry you think so ill of a servant of Jehovah.'

The man spat impatiently over the wall. 'I think ill of him? I just credit him with a bit of common sense.'

'Then I can tell you,' said my father, 'that he has used his own sort of sense in the matter. He has deposited the money in the city treasury for safe keeping, and remains here in the city to await what the Lord sends.'

The man looked him up and down for a moment, noting the delicate hands, the good-quality clothing, and the educated Jerusalem accent. 'You?' he said at last, and laughed. 'Then you have no sort of sense at all, for the man you have just seen making his way out of the gates with his wives and baggage is the city treasurer. Now how do you suppose he managed it?'

I looked from one to the other, too shocked for a moment to grasp the truth. I felt my face redden with rage as it sank in, but my father laughed—a clear, unclouded laugh that made the anxious watchers turn and stare. 'Well!' he said. 'God must be as eager to get rid of his money worries as I am.'

For the moment the expression of contempt still hung on the other man's face, until surprise caught up and left him staring blankly. Then a small friendly grin began to hover about his lips. At that moment, however, our attention was distracted. An uneasy murmur was spreading along the ranks of watchers, arms were pointed towards the oncoming horde, and an old woman gave a tremulous cry of horror. I stared where everyone was staring and saw that the three pale objects I had taken to be forked pennants were the bodies of three men, stripped naked and impaled upon the poles that bore them aloft at the head of Sennacherib's army.

'It will be our scouts,' someone said. There was a flurry of movement behind us, and a woman thrust up the stone steps and elbowed her way to the parapet. She was right beside me, and I could feel the waves of terror and grief that flowed from her like a shudder in the air. I shrank back against my father as she gave a loud strange cry, and then began to sob uncontrollably. Several of the men tried to console her, and lead her away down the steps, but for a long time she would not go, and clung to the parapet watching those three limp shapes bobbing and swaying over the rough ground.

My father drew me close. 'I should have made you go before this,' he said. The laughter had quite gone from his face.

The man who had been speaking to us earlier, turned and put his hand out to check my father as he was about to take me down the steps.

'Not now,' he said. 'Best wait a bit.'

'Why?' said my father.

'Has he no one to go with him?'

'No. He must make his way back to Jerusalem alone.'

The man shook his head. 'I'd say you were a knave as well as a fool,' he said, 'but the Lord looks after his own.'

'You think so?'

'That fellow who rode out just now on his fine horse with his saddlebags stuffed with your Temple money—I reckon he's food for vultures by now.'

'Assyrians? Or bandits?'

'Bandits.'

'How do you know?'

'I've been talking to one of the guards who's come off duty. Some children fled back to the city a half-hour ago. They said there was a band of brigands ambushed just up the road, where the valley narrows. They were fleecing the refugees like sheep—easy as falling off a log, all those defenceless women and children. Only trouble was finding anybody with enough of value to be worth robbing. That fellow with your treasure, now, he'd be a prize worth fighting for.'

'Will they kill him?'

'I wouldn't give much for his chances. Besides, since word got through, people have been holding back. Look at that great crowd now by the the inner gate, waiting. When his party went up the road they'd have been able to give him their full attention. You'd best keep your lad with you a little longer, and let him go with the crowd. It'd be safer.'

'But will they be able to go later? The army will be here very soon.'

I glanced back over the wall; I did not want to see those three poor corpses again, and yet I could not help myself. Faintly drifting up the valley came the wail of horns and the thud of drums, felt rather than heard.

'That's what they're hoping. You wouldn't remember the siege of Samaria, I suppose?'

'No, but I remember Ashdod, and Gath. That was the year Benjamin was born.'

The man glanced at me. 'So long? It seems like yesterday. But I'll tell you something about that campaign. Of course, it was Sargon then, not Sennacherib, but I don't expect their methods have altered much. They never stopped the refugees fleeing an attack—do you know why?'

'I suppose it would distract them from the main attack.'

'Partly that, I daresay,' said the man. 'But the main reason was tactics; what they call psychological warfare. All those women and children, streaming terrified across the country, crying, "The Assyrians are coming! The Assyrians are coming!" Chances were, the next village the army came to would be empty as a dried gourd; they could just march in and take possession without a blow being struck. That's how they come to get across the land so fast.'

'Is that what they're waiting for, all those people down

there?' Below us, at the approaches to the side gate, people and animals swirled and clotted like curds in a churn.

'Some of them, those that have got their wits about them,' said the man. 'I reckon most of them are just waiting for someone to tell them what to do—too scared to go and too scared to stay.'

'Why did the city treasurer go, then, if he already knew about the brigands?' I asked.

'Perhaps no one saw fit to tell him,' said the man. 'If he'd been hanging about in the square, like the poor folk, he'd have heard the rumours. But he wasn't was he? He was in his courtyard, making sure his servants didn't help themselves and give him the slip.'

'The guards must have known,' said my father.

'Oh, aye. But what would they want to tell him for? I bet he paid them a year's wages to let him out through that gate.'

The drums and horns were louder now, and we could hear the jingle of harness and the cries of camel-drivers. I had never seen so many horses and camels in my life before. Few of the soldiers seemed to be on foot; almost all were mounted on something, mostly horses. Today, when I think back all those years, my memory picks up an experience that has lain asleep beneath the folds of time until now. Just for a moment, watching that great army, I forgot I was the victim, waiting like a rat for the snake to strike. I was part of the Assyrian host, in which man was welded to man by training, discipline and singleness of purpose. I knew what it was like to lose my solitariness in an infinitely larger being, so that my own personal danger or pain mattered not at all. I felt I was part of God himself, and my whole spirit flamed with joy.

My eye travelled forward over the might of Assyria till it reached the front; there hung the three naked corpses. Panic pinched out the flame of exaltation. I was no part of that glory, and that god was not my God. My God had ordained us to be victims, as punishment for our sins. My famous grandfather's sermons thundered in my ears. But suppose our God was not as strong as the gods of the Assyrians, and he was just making excuses to my grandfather? Why shouldn't I switch gods?

I crushed that thought as soon as it flashed across my mind, but I knew I was not quick enough. My father need not know, nor the man beside us, but God would know; Jehovah, who sees into the heart of man, would know. It was for just this very sin of disloyalty he was punishing us. Please, God, I did not mean it; forgive me, and save me from the might of my adversary; and save my father from his might, too.

My father must have seen my lips moving in silent prayer, for he put his arm around my shoulders.

'Come,' he said. 'We will go round to the other side, where there are no crowds. We can talk there a little, before you go.'

Desolately, I followed him as he picked his way along the broad walkway that topped the wall behind the parapet, all the way round the city. Once we were out of sight of the advancing army the walls were deserted except for the guards posted at intervals to keep a look-out. When we reached a spot where we could look up the winding valley that led towards Hebron, my father stopped. He helped me scramble up on the parapet, and pulled himself up after me. There we sat in the sunshine, legs swinging, a parody of our carefree travelling days.

Right up in the pass, where the river bed twisted out of sight behind the hills, I could see some movement, but whether of people or animals I could not tell. The road from that point down to the city walls, that had earlier been crowded with fleeing multitudes, now lay deserted, except for one riderless horse that sometimes stooped to snatch a hasty mouthful from the wayside, sometimes trotted towards us, and sometimes stood still, head up, staring uneasily northwards. It looked very like the horse upon which we had seen the city treasurer ride out.

I spoke the thought that had been nagging at me on our walk along the wall.

'If Jehovah has said he is sending the Assyrians to punish us, why do you have to stay and fight? Why does anyone stay and fight? Why don't you all run away and give up the land to the Assyrians, if that's what Jehovah wants?'

'I can't answer that,' said my father. 'Except that, against all reason, a man is ashamed to run away and give up his homeland to the invader. Not everyone, as you very well know, thinks that Grandfather is right.'

'You mean, perhaps we can win, after all?'

'I don't see how we can win,' said my father. 'Assyria is a great empire, and we are a tiny country. Even if we had never split off from the Northern Kingdom, we would still be too weak from a military point of view. It did not take them long to overrun Galilee, and capture Samaria.'

'Do you think if we'd still been one kingdom they'd have conquered us, then, too?'

'If they had, you'd never have known a free Judah. It's twenty-one years since Samaria fell, and with it went three-quarters of Solomon's kingdom.'

I did not know very much about the fall of Samaria because it happened in that gap, too distant for memory but too recent for the history scrolls. What I did know, of course, was that all the country to the north of us, right up to the snow-capped Mount Hermon, was the heritage of us, God's Chosen People. The great King David had conquered it, and the wise King Solomon had ruled it, in the name of Jehovah, in the Golden Age. But as the years passed the dream had turned to a nightmare of bickering over the succession, and of civil war, and the country had fallen apart. Now this little pocket of land called Judah was all the Chosen People could call their own. For how long would that continue?

I knew, too, that after the fall of Samaria, the new King Sargon, whose father, Shalmanezer, had been killed in the battle, herded twenty-seven thousand Israelites into exile in faraway Persia, and replaced them with colonists from Assyria and Babylon. The people who lived across the border from Judah were no longer countrymen. As the Prophet Amos lamented, 'Fallen is the virgin Israel.'

'Listen,' said my father. 'I'm not going to tell you everything will be all right. You know as well as I do that we shall both be beset by great dangers before the day is out. This may be the last time we sit and talk together, and I would like to think we can tell the truth to each other.'

I nodded, for I could not speak.

'I don't know why God has ordained that you and I should be here in Lachish just when the army of Sennacherib comes to destroy it, but so it is. When you are alone and making your way back to Jerusalem, do not forget to repeat all those psalms you have been taught in which we pray to Jehovah to deliver us from our enemies. Pray, because it will be a comfort to you, and you will not feel so lonely. But don't fool yourself. Don't think that if God chooses not to save you, or me, it is because he is weak, or because he hates you. Whether you live or die, you are part of his divine purpose.'

He paused, and I said nothing. All the things I felt like saying would only hurt him, and though I wanted to hurt Jehovah I did not want to hurt my father. Deep down, so deep I hoped God would not hear, my soul cried out curses on him because his divine purpose ought to have been to save my father and me at all costs, and apparently it was not.

'Don't look so down-hearted,' my father went on, quite cheerfully. 'If you keep your wits about you, I see no reason why you should not get safely back to Jerusalem.'

'What good will that be?' I asked. 'The Assyrians will take Jerusalem just as they will take Lachish. What will happen to our family then?'

My father took my hand and held it on his own knee. 'I don't know. But you are my oldest son; I shall feel happier knowing you are there to look after your mother and sisters and little brothers. If you have to flee into the hills, they will need you to find food, and pitch tents, and all sorts of things like that.'

The thought of having to organize that noisy grown-up

household so appalled me that my shoulders must have bowed with the weight, for my father laughed and drew me closer.

'I'm not asking you to make decisions,' he said. 'Your grandfather and uncles will do that, and no doubt your mother will have quite a say in the matter. No, no; they'll know what to do, but they'll need you to help them do it.'

I gave a sigh of relief. 'That's all right then,' I said. 'But. . .' I trailed off, afraid to get the answer to the question in my heart.

My father waited, and I knew that no substitute question would do. 'But you—you don't *know* . . .'

'I don't know that I'll be killed?'

I nodded.

'No. Perhaps we'll all be together again in Jerusalem. But I don't want you to expect that. I want you to face the worst now, while we're together. I don't want to send you away full of false hope only to be alone when the hard time comes. Do you understand that?'

'Yes,' I said. But you can't organize your hopes and despairs to order and although, looking back, I think he was right, at the time it was not much help.

'Remember the dust,' he said. 'I've had thirty-four years in the image of God, and it has been good. If I am called to go back to dust, I hope I shall do it with the praise of God in my heart. It shouldn't be too difficult, when I think of the sons and daughters I have given life to.' He fell into silence, and after a while sighed. Perhaps the thought of his family did not make the prospect of death as easy to bear as he had intended.

'Remember my name,' he said suddenly. 'Remember my ridiculous name.' He smiled, because his name had always been something of a joke among us children. Usually I was the first to tease him about it, but now I just said flatly, 'Why?'

Shear-jashub: "a remnant shall return," it meant. 'Where's that old remnant?' my mother would shout, in jolly mood. 'Hasn't he returned yet?'—when the dinner was ready to serve and my father had not come back from work.

'Because it is important,' said my father. 'I know we always joke about it, but that does not mean it is not important.' Although he spoke quietly, there was an edge of certainty in his voice which reminded me of my prophet grandfather. Usually my father spoke as though he was never quite convinced about anything. In an argument I could not imagine him dismissing the other man's point of view without hesitation. 'Perhaps you are right,' he would concede with a smile, and mean it.

Because of the tone of his voice, memory stirred. I was a small boy, about six, and had not yet learned to be afraid of my grandfather Isaiah. Along with some older boys, I had gone scrambling down the slope of Mount Zion to watch the labourers hacking their way through the rock for the king's great water project. This was to bring fresh water from the Gihon spring, outside the walls, right into the heart of Jerusalem, and it meant tunnelling through 600 metres of solid rock. The tunnel ended in a pool twenty metres below the surface, and flights of steps were being hewn out of the rock to allow the women to come and fill their water pots. Until the work was finished, children were not allowed near that end, because of the danger, but we used to cluster round the spring at Gihon, watching the endless line of sweating workmen bringing out their loads of broken rock. Men were at both ends, and the big question was whether they would really meet, or whether each gang would pass the other in the belly of the earth, and go toiling away for ever into the darkness.

'There he is again,' I heard the foreman say, with a nod towards the hillside opposite, 'disapproving of us, as usual.' I looked across, and saw the solitary figure of a man standing still, watching.

'That prophet?' said the engineer, turning to look.

'Isaiah. Yes, him.'

The engineer grunted, unimpressed, and carried on with his measuring.

Nothing was happening that I hadn't seen many times before, so, as nobody was paying much attention to me, I trotted off down the hill, paddled across the Kidron and scrambled up the rocky slope on the other side. I had lost sight of my grandfather before I crossed the stream, and would probably have forgotten my purpose if I had not suddenly come upon him. He was standing exactly as I had first seen him, and though I scrambled over towards him, sending little cascades of loose shingle pattering down between the ancient olive trunks, in full view of him, he gave no sign of having noticed me.

I pulled his robe, and he looked at me vacantly, as from a great distance.

'Hello, Grandfather,' I said. 'Look where I've climbed.'

I think he probably gave some sort of answer but, childlike, I went on repeating myself until he was forced into paying attention.

'Shear-jashub's boy?' he said eventually.

'I'm Benjamin,' I said. I remember being astonished that anybody whom I recognized should not also recognize me. 'Look where I've climbed. Look.' I grabbed his hand and pointed at the toiling figures on the lower slope opposite.

'Come. I'll take you to the top, then,' he said, and without waiting for an answer he set off up the hillside.

'They won't know where I am,' I said, but he paid no attention, so I supposed it did not matter. After all, he was my grandfather. I slithered and panted along after him, but when we came within sight of the top I ran ahead.

'I got here first!' I shouted.

He ignored that. 'Look!' he said, and pointed north-wards, then swung his arm in a half-circle, slowly, through the east to the south. Nothing but naked brown hills. I suppose there were brown herdsmen following their thin brown goats and sheep in search of pasture, but if there were I did not see them.

My grandfather turned to the west. 'Now look,' he said. Below me was the greyish green of the scattered olives, and below that, the ribbon of green around the Kidron; on the other side, the golden city of David, Jerusalem, crowning the twin Mounts, Zion and Moriah, set here and there with cypress and palm trees, myrtle and juniper.

'By the time you are a man,' he said, 'God may destroy all that city, and make it like those bare hills.'

'All gone?' I asked.

'Not one stone left upon another.'

I don't remember feeling surprise, or fear. The world seemed a safe enough place to me, at six.

'Why?' I asked.

'Because the people who lived there have sinned against Jehovah.'

'All of them?' I asked, with interest. I had no idea what he was talking about.

He did not answer, but stood staring across like a blind man, eyes fixed on a scene that was not there. When he spoke again, it was not to the six-year-old tugging at his robe. 'All have sinned; none have obeyed the voice of the Lord their God.' There was much more, but I don't remember what it was about. I can guess, of course, because Grandfather's message has not altered much over the years. The children of Israel had worshipped other gods, had built idols, had taken bribes, had not cared for the poor, had made themselves rich, had eaten and drunk too much, and had forgotten about the God who had led them out of Egypt five hundred years before.

I suppose I stood around, thinking my own childish thoughts, or played in the dust. Suddenly my attention was caught by a change in his tone, and a familiar name.

'Shear-jashub!' he cried, almost in triumph. 'A remnant shall return!'

'That's my father,' I said.

He paid not the slightest attention. 'The Lord will bring back a remnant of his people, out of captivity, and they shall worship upon his Holy Hill. And it shall come to pass in that day that the remnant of Israel, and such as are escaped of the house of Jacob, shall no more serve their conquerors; but they shall serve the Lord, the Holy One of Israel, in truth.'

'My father?' I said, holding to the only words I could understand.

'I and the children whom God hath given me are for signs and wonders from the Lord of Hosts who dwells in Mount Zion.'

'My father's your son, isn't he?' I asked. 'Did you name him Shear-jashub when he was a baby?' With two younger brothers, I knew all about naming babies.

I don't remember whether he answered me or not. I learnt later that he had chosen the name deliberately, to remind his countrymen that there was an element of hope in the disasters he spent much of his time predicting. He cannot always have been very sure of it himself, because the next time my strange wild grandmother bore him a son he called him Maher-shalal-hash-bas, which means roughly 'the time of pillage and destruction draws on apace'. I scarcely remember Uncle Maher; he died of the same fever that carried off my grandmother the prophetess.

I turned now to my father. 'Yes,' I said. 'I know all about that.' I told him about my childhood memory, and he smiled.

'I think my father has an obsession about that water supply,' he said. 'It was when Hezekiah's father, King Ahaz, wanted to make some improvements that he took me along to tell him it was unnecessary, and he never approved of Hezekiah's great feat, either.'

'I thought he liked King Hezekiah.'

'He does. Getting rid of all corrupt holy shrines up and down the country and purifying the Temple—all that he sees as good. But it's put a lot of backs up—that's why the good people of Lachish were not too pleased to see us, no doubt. It was all right in Bethlehem and Hebron, where they live close enough to the Temple to feel it is their place of worship, but here in Lachish it's all too far away.'

I could not share my father's philosophical attitude

about the Temple dues, so I just said, 'Why doesn't Isaiah approve of the Great Tunnel? Everybody else does. They think it's the greatest thing Hezekiah has ever done.'

'I suppose he feels it is a matter of trusting in ourselves instead of in God. The existing supply, from that open pool at the Gihon spring, is good enough in times of peace. It is only in a seige, when the enemy could cut it off outside our walls, that it would become useless, so Grandfather Isaiah sees it as spending time and money defending ourselves instead of submitting to the will of God.'

'That's silly,' I said. My father did not contradict me, so I went on, 'I mean, why should God want us to sit around like tethered goats waiting for the lion to tear us apart?'

'I don't know,' he said, mildly. 'Perhaps you're right.'

Encouraged, I said, 'If you thought like that, you wouldn't be sending me away to escape the Assyrians. You'd leave it all to God.'

He was silent for quite a long time, and when he spoke again it was as though he shared his soul with me. 'I'm only an ordinary man,' he said. 'Not a prophet. I don't know what God wants—only what other people tell me he wants. Most of the time, that has to be good enough, but now there is something stronger. My heart tells me I must do all I can to save you, because I love you. No other reason. Do you suppose my heart knows God better than my brain?'

How could I answer that? He went on, after a while, 'King Ahaz burnt his own son, his child, as a sacrifice to please God. Did you know that?'

'Yes,' I said.

'He was two or three years old—the same age as I was. He burnt him, to please God.' There was a kind of passion in my father's voice. 'I would rather not please God than do that.'

'But he was wrong,' I cried, more to comfort my father than because I knew anything about it.

'Yes,' he said. 'That's what I believe. If you love me,

you will try to live your life in the belief that the God we worship is not the God of killing, but of saving.'

These were the last words I remember of my father's. Of course, we had more conversation as we walked back into the throng and made what few plans it was possible to make, but it was all surface talk, and the words have drifted away like smoke.

In the dusty square at the foot of the great wall, people and animals milled restlessly. Two guards stood at the small gate by which the refugees hoped to leave; other armed men pushed their way impatiently through the crowds, carrying equipment and missiles for the great catapults set up on platforms behind the parapets; archers were ordered here and there, and other orders were shouted from housetop to street, and from street to lookout post. Some young boys strutted after the soldiers, laughing and shouting, but the small children mostly huddled in families, bewildered and frightened, and the older ones could not be called down from the walls. Some of the women shouted and fretted, others just stood, dumb with fright. Even down below, we could hear the drumbeats and the wailing horns of the approaching army.

Up above, the archers and the catapult crews stood at their posts in readiness to shoot, but we could hear the order, relayed from tower to tower, that no weapon was to be loosed until the Assyrians either parleyed, or attacked. Everyone knew that once the battle was joined, there could be only one end. Any chance, however slim, of coming to terms was not to be thrown away by some hothead hurling puny defiance at the giant army. But the enemy must now be very near, and an angry mutter ran round the walls, swelling to a reverberating moan. My father was talking to the guards at the gate, and I ran up the steps, along with many others, to see what was happening.

What I saw left me breathless, drowning in fear.

The whole of the valley beneath, to right and left, was filled with men and horses, and still there seemed no end to the broad column that marched along the roadway from the north. Indeed, further back, soldiers could be seen dismounting from their horses, leaving them tethered in lines and coming forward to take up their positions on foot, each one armed with a wicker shield and bronze helmet, and carrying either a lance or a great curved bow. These were marching steadily forward and taking their places in front of the horsemen. In the centre, a pathway was left clear for the approach of gangs of slaves dragging what appeared to me to be quantities of tree trunks. Behind them, stout wooden engines, like huge boxes with strong poles protruding from the front, jolted over the ground on wheels. I could not see what moved these, because neither beasts nor men were pulling them. Far back, strings of camels meandered along with their undulating stride until led to the sides of the valley to be unloaded of the supplies piled on their backs. The cries of the camel-drivers drifted clearly over the nearer rumble and clink of the armed forces, for now the drums and horns had fallen silent.

Now, too, I saw what had caused the moans of rage from our men on the outer wall below us. I had just been able to see, over the top of the outer wall, where some Assyrians stood holding a single great wicker shield, wide enough to protect three or four men at once from our bowmen on the walls immediately above them. What was going on behind the shield I could not tell, but now an order was shouted, men withdrew down the hillside with picks and shovels, and others came forward, raising once more those three pale, naked corpses transfixed on poles. One by one, the poles were hoisted into position, and slotted into the prepared holes, and there the grim trophies dangled before the eyes of their own townsfolk, until they rotted and fell to the ground for the bones to be picked clean by scavenging jackal and vulture. By then, the scavengers were spoiled for choice, for the battle of Lachish was over and done, and only the dead of both sides remained to tell the story.

It was the human jackals, the brigands who had kept the

refugees bottled up inside the city all this time, whom the people of Lachish were cursing now. They had waited and waited, in the hope that the jackals would scurry off to their lair as the Assyrian lion approached; but they had waited too long, and now it was too late. It seemed that the whole city was surrounded by the enemy, rank upon rank of them, just keeping out of range of the bowmen and the catapult crew. It would be a brave woman now who would venture out of the postern gate to scramble down the hillside between the opposing armies and thrust her way among the ranks of the attackers. Some began to go back to their houses, others found a foothold on the inner wall, the rest went up to the housetops to watch and wait.

By this time, the defending soldiers had taken up their positions on the outer wall, except for the catapult crews. These great engines of war were too bulky to be sited on the comparatively small towers of the outer wall, and keeping them supplied with stones would be difficult and dangerous in that position. Instead, they were anchored on the larger platform behind the inner towers that guarded each angle of the wall, so that invaders who managed to scale the outer wall would find themselves enclosed in a belt of bare hillside under the constant battering of stones from these weapons. The main activity round the inner wall at this time centred around these towers, as sweating labourers piled up heaps of stones on the six-metre-wide wall on either side of the towers, ready for firing. Any tumble-down shed was seized upon and demolished to provide ammunition, and in many of the poorer houses the women stood in their doorways, fearful lest their homes should literally be pulled down about their ears.

I went back down to my father, and we walked together to the centre of the city, where all the main buildings stood in a square round an open courtyard. This was where the business and government of the city was carried on: on one side was the treasury where my father had sought a safe hiding-place for the Temple dues; on another, the houses of the rulers and priests; next, great storehouses; and finally the site of the High Place, the centre of local worship which Hezekiah had ordered to be destroyed. In the courtyard, women and men alike were gathering cloth in great heaps, and winding strips of material round stakes. These were dispatched in bundles to the outer defences, there to be plunged in huge jars of oil, ready to be set alight and hurled at the attackers.

We passed out of the glare of the open yard and into a store house, where it was cool and dark, but no quieter. Here, too, women were tearing cloth into strips, for bandages this time; others were using bedding to fashion rough stretchers with whatever stakes they could save from the soldiers. Tall jars of wine and water and oil stood ready to wash and anoint the wounded. One man, whom I took to be a doctor, examined his tools; another sharpened a long-bladed knife on a grindstone.

This was the place my father was looking for, and he went over to speak to the doctor, who was glad enough to find someone who knew a little medicine offering his services. Soon there would be plenty of work, but now, as for everyone else, there was little to do but wait.

There was a sudden flurry of movement outside, and someone shouted that the Assyrian Commander-in-chief was coming out to parley.

But in fact there was no parley. By the time we reached the walls, the Rabshakeh, the Assyrian Commander-in-chief, was riding back down the hill. The terms he had offered were total submission; the men of Lachish must open their gates and give themselves up as prisoners and slaves.

The gates remained closed.

Evidently the Rabshakeh had expected no less, for at once preparations for an assault began.

Now it had seemed to me that although the Assyrians were bound to win in the end simply because there were so many of them, actually to take Lachish by storm would be impossible. Apart from a narrow postern to the east, there was only one gate in the outer wall. This stood half-way up the steep hillside, on ground so rough that any attack on it would be practically impossible. Moreover, once through it, the invaders would find themselves in a narrow steep roadway with thick high walls on either side, leading straight up the hill to the second gateway. This was the only link between the two walls. All the rest of the way round the town they were separated by a wide, steep, unbroken belt of bare hillside overlooked by the massive wall of the inner defences. The refugees had been leaving by a very narrow gate cut in the thickness of the six-metre-wide inner wall, which let them through into the connecting roadway, at the foot of which they had to go down narrow steps cut diagonally through the gatehouse wall, so that they eventually emerged below, and at the side of, the main gate. Anybody trying to rush this gate would have to fight their way up a series of inner stairways and passages where only two men could stand abreast.

The outer main gate was enormously thick and strong, and was now blocked up on the inside with stones and sandbags. Moreover, it was set in a square tower, topped by a parapet which encircled an area big enough to accommodate a large number of defenders, and supplies of rocks and firebrands to hurl down on any attackers bold enough to try a direct assault upon the entrance below.

One weakness had become evident, however, when the Assyrians had advanced and set up those poles with their grisly burdens. Because there were no catapults on the outer defences, the only weapons the defenders could project more than a man's throw from the walls were arrows, and, though none were fired at that time, the enemy had obviously felt they were sufficiently protected from these by the great wicker shield behind which they had worked.

It became obvious soon enough that the attackers had taken this into account. Flanked by a continuous wall of well-armoured soldiers carrying these great shields, scores upon scores of poor ragged creatures—slaves, they appeared to me—came forward dragging the logs I had seen earlier. While soldiers dug more holes and inserted supporting uprights into these, the slaves piled log upon log between them, to create a solid ramp, rising to some four metres above ground level, which crawled inexorably towards the great outer gate.

'Why the gate?' I asked a young soldier. With such a ramp they could make a pathway clear to the top of the encircling wall at any point between the towers; why choose the most stoutly defended spot, and where the parapet stood too high for the ramp to surmount?

'They need our roadway to build upon, most probably,' he said. 'And the angle of the hill is less steep there than anywhere else.'

His companion, an older man, shook his head. 'Maybe,' he said. 'But it's the gatehouse they're after. Breasting the wall wouldn't do them much good—they'd be sitting targets for our engines here, and would have no means of getting fresh supplies of weapons. But once they've taken the gatehouse, it will be a different story. They'll have protection from our weapons, and a storehouse for their own.'

'They'll never do it,' said the young soldier, but he was wrong.

As soon as the work brought them within range, the defenders began to hurl stones and firebrands down, and arrows flew like hail. We could see little of the effect because the gate-tower itself was in the way, but the cries of the wounded and dying filled the air. What we could see were the Assyrian soldiers herding more and yet more slaves to carry on with the building. Few returned.

'We're only slaughtering our own people,' muttered the older guard.

'Judaeans?' I cried, horrified. 'These labourers?'

'Very likely; Samarians, Philistines; could be from their conquests in the north.'

As we watched, we saw a ragged fellow, streaming with blood, running away back down the hill. Casually, a young officer drove his lance through his body and, wrenching it out again, did not even stoop to see if the wretch was dead.

'Little they care how many we kill,' remarked the guard. 'It will save them feeding them tonight, and tomorrow they can use us instead—those of us who are still alive.'

The young soldier stared at him. 'I'd rather die!' he cried.

'You could get lucky,' remarked the other, drily. 'They're calling for us now.'

Casualties were not all on the Assyrian side. A good many of their covering volleys of arrows found their mark among the defenders on the gatehouse, and batches of soldiers on the inner defences were waiting their turn to take the places of the dead. More than once, I had seen my father go down the roadway to the gatehouse and help bring back the wounded; the dead were thrown over the wall.

Now we could see that the slaves were no longer carrying up logs, but sacks of earth, and small stones and turf, which they emptied on the ramp and stamped in between the holes of the tree trunks, to make an even surface ready to take the wheeled battering rams.

There were three of these, and they had been manoeuvred into position at the foot of the ramp. I could see now that they were like carts with barrel-shaped roofs and no floor; and each was big enough to contain some half-dozen or more soldiers, safe from attack. Only a direct hit by a massive rock looked likely to shatter those stout wooden frames. In front of each, a single pole stuck out in the manner of an ox-cart shaft but a great deal more massive. There must have been some sort of struts inside for each soldier to push on, for when the order came each machine rolled up the incline with extraordinary speed and force. They did indeed charge like a great angry ram.

Suddenly, my father appeared at my side.

'You must go,' he said. He was streaked with sweat and dirt and blood, and his frame shook a little from the unaccustomed exertion, but his voice was steady enough.

'Now?' I said, astonished.

'Yes,' he said. 'Look!'

I looked where he pointed, away to the left of the gatehouse, and saw groups of women and children, huddling together as they stumbled round the flank of the hill on what was little more than a goat track, making for the further reaches of the Hebron road, beyond the point where it was filled with the massed Assyrian forces. Arrows flew over their heads from the bowmen on the walls, but they were very soon out of the direct line of fire, which was concentrated entirely on the ramp. The Assyrians had presumably been ordered not to attack them directly, though I saw one laughing bowman deliberately shooting into the fleeing crowd. A child screamed and fell, and was picked up by his mother and hauled away; an old man crumpled, and was left lying beside the path. An officer shouted at the archer, who shrugged and turned back to the defenders on the walls.

'It has to be now,' said my father. 'As soon as the gatehouse falls, there will be no way out.'

'Will it fall so soon?' someone asked. 'They will never batter down such thick walls with those machines.'

My father shook his head. 'I've just come from the gatehouse,' he said. 'Those engineers know what they are doing. The top of the ramp comes about the height of a man below the top of the parapet.' He shuddered. 'I think the last few metres needed no logs of wood. The ramp is filled up with dead bodies, and the stones our soldiers have been hurling down. But the parapet behind which our men are sheltering is not nearly as thick as the main walls of the tower, and when the enemy send their battering rams up the ramp, they will strike the wall just at the base of the parapet. I do not think it can be long before they breach it and come pouring through.'

His words produced considerable alarm around us, but he was not the only man to bring the news back from the gatehouse. Great gangs of soldiers now began to take up positions on and around the inner gate, and those who were not there to fight were unceremoniously shoved out of the way.

'Come,' said my father.

Together we climbed down into the throng now madly trying to cram through the tiny doorway. I saw old men pushed to the ground, children thrust from their mothers, precious bundles split and their contents tumbled among the feet of the mob. After the hours of indecision and delay, it seemed that life itself was less important than getting first out of that city.

My father had business to take him through. He wore the sash of a medical orderly, and the guards forced the crowd back to make way for him. I followed in his wake. Together we ran down the roadway, but at the foot of it there was no time for leave-taking. His way lay up into the gatehouse to drag back any wounded who could be saved before it fell; mine down the dark narrow steps and out into a world of terror, alone.

Chapter 2

Of course, I was not really alone. Streams of terrified people surged all around me. A few hours before, I had glimpsed the thrill of belonging to a great victorious army, imagining myself part of a single, united force; now I knew what it was like to be part of a panic-stricken mob. A single impulse shuddered through us all, the mindless, pitiless compulsion to flee. I could no more have acted for myself than if I had been one muscle in the frame of a maddened bullock that has broken free from the ropes drawing it to the place of slaughter and gone careering through the city streets, eyes glazed and staring. I trod upon the dead and dying of both sides; when a wayward lance struck the woman in front of me, I pushed her aside and hurried on.

We could not circle the hill beneath the wall for ever, or we should have returned to our starting point. Sooner or later we had to veer down into the village.

Assyrians, though, were everywhere. It was not now the fighting men we had to face, but all the back-up forces that accompany an army on the move. Here were lines of fine Arab horses and their grooms, and beyond, bevies of men lighting fires and setting out rations of food. Camels browsed where they could, or waited patiently to be unloaded of the great packs strapped on their humps. Engineers were digging water holes in the river bed, and tents were being set up wherever the ground was flat enough. Young corn and fields of cucumbers were being trampled into the ground.

The fact that I remember these things must show that the first blind panic was ebbing. We had gasped and scrambled our way for a mile or more and the sound of battle was fading. All the same, we heard the sudden shouts and the wailing of the horns and knew the gatehouse had been taken. Soon, looking back, we could see the end of the long line of fleeing refugees. Anyone left in the city now was doomed to death or slavery.

A group of men, camel-drivers and the like, had gathered in our path. They watched the wretched cavalcade with amused contempt, every now and again falling upon a pretty girl, and passing her between themselves to be mocked and embraced before being allowed to go weeping on her way.

If they saw anything that looked worth stealing, they stole it. I, a small boy with nothing except a few coins tied up in my belt, was allowed to pass unmolested.

The fear of greater danger drives out the fear of a lesser. It was only after the people round me had passed the last of the Assyrian host that they began to talk about brigands. The sun was slipping down to the west; it lay warm on our backs, but where the track wound between the hills ahead, shadow filled the valley. In our land, evenings are short; half an hour from sunset to dark. We had come down from Hebron to Lachish, my father and I, easily in one day, but then we had started at dawn, and had animals to ride. This straggle of laden women, old men and children had left Lachish well past noon, already worn out by fear and uncertainty, and had no hope of reaching shelter before night; and the further they fled from the Assyrians, the greater the danger of being set upon by the bandits lurking in the hills.

Most of the refugees, however, seemed to feel the bandits were a lesser danger. At least they were a familiar hazard, something travellers accepted as part of life. Outlaws and murderers they might be, but they spoke the same language and belonged to the same race as the rest of us, and were ruled by the same God.

'It's only our money they'll be after, not our lives,' said one woman. 'And they'll find precious little of that.'

A tired-looking mother, lagging under the weight of a baby as well as a bundle of possessions, and with two young children trailing after her, said, 'If our men are killed and our money stolen, they may as well kill me, and my children. The knife is quicker than starvation.'

An old man turned on her. 'Two years ago,' he said, 'my son's family were attacked by bandits. He was killed, and a good many others, but his daughter—pretty little thing she was, about the age of this lad here—she was taken away. We never heard of her again.'

A silence, weary as death, fell on the straggle of refugees. The sands of exhaustion sucked in the panic that had coursed so strongly through us and we drifted irresolutely to a halt.

'I want to sleep,' wailed a child.

The old man laid a hand on my sleeve. 'Help me to that rock,' he said, and I put my arm under his shoulder and lowered him down. He held out his arms to the wailing child, one of three belonging to the woman who had spoken earlier. 'Come,' he said, simply. The girl stumbled into his arms, and lay back against him, limp as a rag doll. Only the dark eyes were alive, watching her mother anxiously under the drooping eyelids. The mother moved to one side to be near her, still clutching the baby, and the third child, a boy of about seven, trailed after, holding on to her dress. The string of refugees trudged on past, closing the little gap we had left, drawn on in their weariness by the simple instinct to follow.

We belonged with them no more. By the act of stepping a couple of metres off the track, the old man had given our little group a new entity. We were separate; we could make up our own minds what to do. An old man, a woman and three small children, and myself. For the first time since I had left my father, I felt a sense of loyalty; we were friends, we six, although I had said no word to any of them.

Nobody spoke for a long while. I sat down on the dusty

ground, and the boy copied me, still pulling at his mother's dress. She stayed standing, but sagged sideways with the weight of the child on her hip, too weary even to make a decision to rest. It was not that we had come far; but terror had stalked her through the long hours since daybreak, not letting her go or stay, work or rest, eat or think, with the children pulling at her and her husband torn from her to face almost certain death.

'There is no need to go further,' the old man said at length. 'It will be as safe to stay here, and make the journey to Hebron tomorrow.'

'We are too near the Assyrian army,' said the woman. 'Wake the child. We must go on.'

'In an hour it will be dark, and we shall be in bandit country. This child can go no further.'

The woman's eyes rested silently on me.

'I could carry her,' I said. I thought it was kindness, but really, I just wanted to belong.

'As you will,' said the old man. 'Me, I stay here.'

'*Here*?' asked the seven-year-old, suddenly attentive. He looked around at the naked landscape. Above, the valley narrowed between the overshadowing hills; behind, the track by which we had come wound between vineyards and standing young corn, for the area around Lachish itself was well watered; but most of the crops had been trampled by the invading army, and ancient olive trees hacked to pieces for firewood. We had stopped in a kind of no-man's land between the cultivated valley and the bare hillsides; below us, near the stream bed, a strip of tangled and neglected cucumber plants sprawled around a rough stone shelter, erected probably for the benefit of some old man whose job it was to tend and water the crop, and drive off marauding goats. On the higher slopes, rock roses and asphodel glimmered in the fast-fading light.

'We could sleep in that shed,' I said. The 'we' passed without comment. I realized the old man thought I was part of the woman's family, and she probably assumed I was with my grandfather.

'The soldiers may come up here in the night,' said the woman.

'They have no reason to,' answered the old man. 'Their business is with Lachish.' He handed the sleeping child to me. She whimpered a little, and flung her two arms up in sudden alarm, but soon dropped back into sleep, her head on my shoulder. The old man got up slowly, grasping at the older boy for support, and we began to make our way over the rough ground to the shed. I was used to carrying small children around, being third in a family of five, but only in play; I found it difficult to keep my footing while supporting the limp form and lolling head of the sleeping girl. In the end I found it easier to hold her cradled in my arms, but by the time we reached the shed I was staggering and breathless.

The mother smiled at me as we paused at the dark entrance. 'You're a good boy,' she said. 'Lay her down here against the wall.' She stooped to go in, and was nearly knocked down by a couple of terrified goats as they stampeded out of the narrow entrance. The baby burst into hiccuping wails which woke the girl, who cried too, and over the sudden din we heard the despairing shout of the older boy.

'Mum!' he cried. 'Help me!'

The woman swung round in sudden alarm, but it was only that the old man, his hand on the lad's shoulder, had fallen so far behind that his reluctant helper had begun to panic.

'Go, you,' said the woman.

As soon as I reached them, the boy belted off like a scared lamb after its mother. The old man's progress was certainly very slow, and the arm across my shoulders trembled. His breath came in rasping gasps.

'Are you all right?' I asked. He did not answer till we had reached the shed and he stood, wheezing and bent, resting his shoulder against the wall until he could gather the strength to stoop into the entrance. The woman and the three children were already huddled inside.

'Right enough,' he said. 'Right enough for all I have left to do.'

'What's that?' I asked.

'Die,' he said.

I was not sure I had caught the word, let out softly on a rattling breath, so I pretended I had not heard.

He looked slowly around. 'Man and boy,' he said, 'I've worked this land.'

'Here?' I asked. 'Is this your field?'

'My family's,' he said. He stroked a stone in the wall. 'I built this, I and my father, when I was a lad of your age,' he said. 'I've worked these fields, and gathered these crops, and carried them back to the city, and sat in the market place with the gourds and cucumbers piled in front of me as high as this shed—in good years, that is. I've seen my children grow thin in the bad years. . . .' He did not finish the sentence, but gazed down the valley at the smoking bonfire that was Lachish. 'My land, and my city. Where else would a man wish to die, when his time comes?'

'Come inside, and rest,' I said.

It was very dark inside the shed, and it smelled of dried goat dung. A contented sucking noise told me the woman had her baby at her breast. Out of the darkness, the boy's voice spoke.

'When's supper?' he asked.

I laughed. I could not help it.

'Oh, Joel!' the woman cried, laughing too, but the laughter turned to a burst of stormy weeping. A little silence fell upon the children as their mother's sobs died away, and then the girl said, 'I'm hungry, too.'

In my bag I had some bread, and olives, and a handful of dried figs. They were all I had to last till I got home to Jerusalem. I was hungry, too, but if I would not share, I could not eat.

The old man said, 'I have a little bread, which I do not want. The children can have it, and if this boy were to go and look before it gets too dark, he might find some cucumbers.'

'I have meal cakes,' the woman said, 'and a jar of oil.' Our eyes were growing accustomed to the dark, and I saw her turn her head doubtfully towards me. 'If I share,' she said, 'the little ones will go hungry before we reach Hebron. I thought you were with the old man.'

'No,' I said. 'I am alone. And I have food, too.' I started to unknot my bundle, but laid it by when the boy, Joel, said, 'Let's go and look for cucumbers.'

We scrambled out together, I and the small boy, who until a few minutes ago would not leave go of his mother's dress. Now I was one of the family.

After the darkness of the shed, it seemed quite light outside, but it was still difficult to find the curved green cucumbers among the curving stalks and furled leaves. It was best, I discovered, to pick out the faint yellow stars of the flowers, and then fumble back down the stalks to the ripening fruits that grew near the main stem. Joel picked more than I did, but very small ones; once it would have been a waste, but now it scarcely mattered. They would be stolen, or destroyed, soon enough, by the Assyrian army.

We returned with our treasure to find a flickering light glowing within the dark entrance. The woman had contrived a torch by binding a strip of material round a stick, dipping it in the oil, and wedging it between two stones. It would not last long, but long enough for us to set out our supplies and divide them between us, setting half aside for the next day. The ring of faces glowed in the flame that, as it alternately flared up or dimmed, invested them with an illusion of animation—here a quick shadowed grin, there a sparkle in the eyes. We chewed the bread and crunched the cucumbers in companionable silence. It felt like an evening at home after a long exhausting day.

The tiny shed scarcely allowed room for us all to sit, and when I tried to lie back against the wall, a clatter of tools fell about my ears. The handle of the hoe struck the little girl, who screamed, but she was not badly hurt.

'Hush, now, Rebecca,' the woman said, and I asked the

old man if I could put the tools outside, for I presumed they were his.

He had been sitting with head bowed, eating very little, and now that I looked at him I could see his lips moving, as in prayer, but slowly and stiffly. I repeated the question, as he did not seem to have heard me, and he raised his eyes and stared at me blankly for a while, before answering. 'Aye, put the old spade outside. He won't come to harm, this one night.'

As I tried to bundle up the four or five implements without hitting anybody in that crowded space, the old man put out his hand. 'Let me have him a moment,' he said.

'The spade?'

He did not answer, and I could not disentangle one tool from another, so I carried them all out, propped the rest against the wall, and brought the spade back in. I saw then that the iron blade was worn away to little more than a sliver, and the wooden handle gleamed in the flame, polished and moulded by the countless hours of shared labour, man and tool. He still held out his hand, and I laid the handle in the outstretched palm. The old fingers closed stiffly round the silk-smooth shaft, each one finding a familiar and invisible groove.

I stood, bent beneath the low roof, waiting for him to release it, but the woman said, 'Leave it with him; we'll manage.'

Just then, the light suddenly flared up, and died, and total darkness engulfed us. Rebecca gave another startled wail, and Joel said, 'Can you make another candle, Mum?' But there was no point in that. Our meal was over, and all we needed now was sleep.

Trying to remember exactly where everybody was, I gently lowered the spade, still clutched in the old man's hand, and felt about for a space to lie down.

'Is that you, Joel?' I asked, touching hair.

'Yes,' he said, 'and I'm not at all comfy.'

I lay down beside him, next to the doorway. The old

man was opposite me, and his feet reached almost to my chin. I could not straighten my own legs in the narrow width of the shed, but Joel was all right; he could just manage to lie at full stretch. Opposite him, and next to the old man, his mother shifted about, trying to find a way to rest curled round her baby. The little girl, Rebecca, was uneasy. She was wedged between Joel and the far wall, and she would rather have been alongside her mother.

'Where are you, Mum?' she kept whimpering, and Joel grunted at her impatiently to stop fidgeting. He was the first to drop asleep though, for unlike Rebecca he had not slept earlier. The baby, too, slept contentedly enough then; full of his mother's milk, and swaddled in his blanket, he dreamed on in his own cocooned world. Whether the old man slept or woke, I could not tell. The wheezy uneven breathing went on and on, interspersed with mutterings whose words I could not make out, but the rhythms sounded like the Psalms.

The illusion of homeliness had gone out with the light. I lay and stared at the rectangle of sky. It was a very dark night, with no moon, and too overcast for stars, so the silhouette of hills scarcely showed; but to the south the glow of enemy camp fires shone in the mist, and a faint but continuous clamour drifted up the valley. Was my father resting now, and thinking of me? Was he too busy in the hospital? Was he a prisoner? Was he dead?

A terrible loneliness clutched at me, and I held my breath and listened to the sounds close around. Only from the woman's corner came complete silence, and I felt sure that she, too, was lying wide-eyed and enduring. I was twelve years old, and she was not my mother; I could not wail like Rebecca, but I shifted about urgently and noisily, not as one shifts when asleep.

'Are you cold, son?' came the voice from the corner. I paused a moment, and then said, 'I think Joel's asleep.'

'It's you I meant,' she said. 'But I don't know your name.'

'Benjamin,' I said. 'I'm all right.' I was a bit cold, although I had wrapped my travelling blanket around me.

'I thought, at first, you were with the old man—his grandson, perhaps.'

We talked quietly in the darkness. I explained how I came to be among the refugees, alone, and learned that her name was Hannah, and she was the wife of Joash, the potter. Her own people were from the Northern Kingdom, Samaria, and she hoped to make her way there, to be among them.

'That is where Joash will look for me,' she said, 'if he lives. But we do not know if any of my people still live there, or whether they were carried away into captivity when the Assyrians first conquered the Northern Kingdom.'

Talking eased my fear and loneliness, and soon after I must have fallen asleep.

I was woken some hours later by the sound of crying—the harsh angry roars of a baby with colic.

'Oh, shut up, Reuben,' muttered Joel beside me, burrowing back into sleep; and I remembered exactly the feeling, when I was a child of seven and my youngest brother was a three-month-old infant. A bit of a moon had risen and, though veiled behind thin cloud, cast enough light for me to discern the outline of Hannah, rocking her baby and whispering soothing words to him. It had no effect. She put him to her breast, but either she had no milk for him, or he was not hungry, for after a moment's silence he began to wail again.

But in the short space of quietness, we heard something that drove all thoughts of sleep away. It was the sound of raucous, tuneless singing, broken by bursts of drunken laughter, and it was not far away.

'Hush, oh hush!' whispered the mother, thrusting the baby's face into her bosom as if to force him to feed and be quiet, but he wriggled his neck around angrily, giving half-smothered sobs.

'What's the matter, Mum?' Rebecca's voice echoed

clearly in the tiny space, and we all hushed her fiercely, which made her start to cry too.

'Come, my little one,' said the old man out of the darkness. Sleep must have revived him for his voice, though soft, was composed and strong. 'Your mother is nursing the baby; come and sit by me. We have to be quiet, for there are strangers around.'

The girl stumbled over our legs; when she came by the door, I could see her tousled hair, and her thumb still sleepily in her mouth. The baby shook his head free and gave a single loud wail before his mother could stifle it, and the singing and laughing stopped abruptly. Someone spoke—it sounded like a question—and another voice answered, and after a pause the singing started again.

'I'll take a look,' I whispered.

'Me too,' said Joel.

'No!' muttered his mother. 'Just Benjamin. And be careful!'

I crept out and peered round the angle of the shed. I was safe enough for I crouched in the shadow, but it did not need the half-moon to show me the group of five men making their wavering way along the track above us, for one of them held a flaring torch. Another seemed to be carrying a great knife, which he jabbed about wildly in the air, the blade bright in the torchlight.

'Oh, shut your racket!' exclaimed one—I thought it was the man with the knife, but could not be sure. 'You'll scare off every sheep for miles.'

'Roast mutton!' scoffed another. 'Whose daft idea was it anyhow, to look for sheep in the pitch dark?'

'That's the way you catch 'em, see?' said the knife-man, and suddenly, with a wild yell, he launched himself upon a pale humped object by the path. There was a clatter and a stream of oaths; it was the rock the old man had rested upon that the drunkard had mistaken for a sheep. The other men lolled against each other, bellowing with laughter, but it was cut short when the victim scrambled to his feet and turned upon them in a fury with the knife.

Into that silence fell a piercing wail from Reuben.

The quarrel forgotten, all the men turned and stared into the dark valley.

I backed away into the doorway.

'They've heard that!' I whispered. 'There's five of them—drunk—but one's got a knife. And they've got a torch.'

'Are they coming this way?' asked Hannah.

'I don't know. I think so.' I scrambled out again. At first I thought all the group were still standing on the track, arguing, but then I caught a glint of metal below them, and I realized only four men stood round the torch. The knife-man had begun to fumble his way towards the shed.

'Take the children, and go,' said Hannah, when I told them what I had seen. 'Try not to let them see you, but if they do see you, run!'

'She's right,' said the old man, as I hesitated. 'It's the safest way.'

'Aren't you coming?' said Joel to his mother. 'Why aren't you coming? I don't want to go without you.'

'I don't want to go without you,' repeated Rebecca, not at all sure what it was all about.

'Yes, I'm coming,' said Hannah, 'but you go first. And quickly. And don't make a sound. Now, at once.'

Cowed by the tone in her voice, they crept out after me. We crouched for a moment in the shadows, the safe bulk of the shed between us and the Assyrians, while I considered which was the best way.

'Into the stream bed,' said the old man. 'Upstream. There are good places to hide.'

As I pulled little Rebecca after me, wondering if the shed would hide us from the soldiers all the way to the lip of the gully, it flashed across my mind that it would be dead easy to save myself if I were not lumbered with this stranger's children.

'Is Mummy coming?' said Rebecca.

'Ssh. Yes.' But I knew she would not. There would be no point in her running away unless she left her crying baby behind. Reuben had ceased his loud wailing, but still erupted into choking sobs from time to time, as a baby does that has cried itself into exhaustion. As for the old man, he would have to take his chance.

We made it safely to the gully—safely, but not quickly. Loose stones tumbled under our feet as we slid down, and I heard exclamations from the men, and saw the torch held aloft for an instant before the bank hid me.

'There go your sheep,' said one man.

'Goats, more likely,' said another.

'I want to know what's in that shed, any road,' said a third.

The language was strange to me, but near enough to Aramaic for me to understand. Joel had understood too, for he swung round, the moonlight on his frightened face, as though to turn back.

'Go on,' I said, pushing him. 'Do as your mother said.'

I did not dare think what would happen when the soldiers came to the shed. I just knew I wanted to get the children as far away as possible before it did happen.

Speed was more important than caution, for the soldiers were making too much noise themselves, stumbling and swearing over the rough ground, to hear any noise that we might make. From the shed itself we could hear nothing now.

The stream bed was not quite dry; a few small pools of water lurked between the stones, but they were not enough to hinder our progress. What concerned me more was that the banks were getting shallower, and we would soon be scrambling over stones more or less level with the surrounding ground. However, what I had not realized was that we had been following a curved course, and when I looked back I could see that the slope of the hill would very soon cut between us and the shed. For about twenty metres we had to walk in full view of the torch carried by the soldiers, but there was little danger that they would notice us, for we carried no light, and their own light would blind them to the darkness all around.

Joel kept glancing round. 'Where's mother?' he asked, several times. 'I don't see her.'

'She'll be hiding somewhere else,' I said.

'Reuben will cry,' he said, and looked up at me with a face full of fears. I knew he was not deceived. But a moment later, when Rebecca took up the cry, 'Where's Mummy?' he replied scornfully. 'Don't be silly; she's coming later,' and she was content.

It was not long, though. We had scarcely squatted down behind some rocks round the angle of the hill, when there was a sudden burst of shouting, the sound of blows, a man moaning, and a single, fearful, scream. Then silence, before the men's voices rose again, in a ragged chorus of laughter and triumph, not quite loud enough to drown the noise of a woman weeping.

Rebecca crouched, dumb as a terrified curlew chick, but Joel leapt up and would have run all the way back if I had not caught him by the foot and brought him headlong to the ground.

'What did you do that for?' he gasped, beating at me with his fists. 'Let go! Let me go!'

Luckily the men were making too much noise to be able to hear Joel, but still I clamped my hand roughly over his mouth while pressing him tightly to the ground. My violence was an echo of my own fear, and it cowed him utterly. His eyes over my cupped hand stared up at me wildly, and when after a few moments I relaxed my hold, he lay on his back on the ground, trembling from head to foot, his mouth open, but no sound coming from it. He appeared to have stopped breathing, and I stared back at him in consternation, fearing that he was possessed by the devil.

But what I found scaring seemed to bring little Rebecca to her senses. She looked at her brother, arched and prostrate on the ground, for a few moments and then said calmly, 'He's holding his breath. You must shake him, to get the devil out. That's what Mummy does.'

Gingerly, I lifted the stiff small body, and gave it a

gentle shake. 'Harder,' said Rebecca. She grabbed him by the shoulders and pummelled them to and fro with all her tiny strength, and after a minute Joel drew in a great rasping breath and flung himself over on his face, crying. Rebecca sat herself beside him and stroked his dark hair. 'Poor Joel,' she said. 'Poor Joel.' She seemed not the least bit frightened by Joel's devil, and his troubles filled her mind shutting out all else. It was as though she had never heard that terrible scream, those blows and moans. Joel could not have forgotten, but he was, for the moment, empty and defeated. They drew more comfort from each other than they could get from me and, indeed, I had no comfort to give.

I sat down a little way off, staring glumly at the children in the moonlight, and thought. The last sounds of the drunken gang were fading away into the distance. They were going home, and if I dreaded to think what they were taking with them, I dreaded more the thought of finding what they had left behind. As I sat there, a simple solution to all my problems slipped sweetly into my mind.

'Rebecca,' I said. 'I am going back to look for your mother. You are to stay here with Joel till I come back. You are not to move, do you understand?'

'Yes,' she said. 'Stay with Joel.'

'That's right,' I said. This was going to be easier than I thought.

Unexpectedly, Joel spoke, almost into the ground. 'Tell her to be quick,' he said. 'I want her now.'

I was taken aback. A few minutes ago, Joel understood everything; now, it seemed, he understood nothing. Looking back, I realized that a man's mind—or a child's mind, for that matter—has tricks to protect itself, just as the body has, and one of its tricks is simply not to recognize the truth when the truth is too painful to bear.

'Yes,' I said. 'Goodbye, now.' I walked quickly away down the hillside, not bothering to take cover in the stream bed. I rounded the hill, and saw, far away down the track, a single flickering torch bobbing about in the darkness that lay between me and the encamped army. I could see Lachish itself from here. Lights shone from there, too, high up on the hill-top, and columns of fiery smoke rose up into the night sky from burning buildings; while down below in the encircling valley pinpricks of clearer flame marked the army camp fires. Just below me, I could make out the pale mound of the shed in its garden of cucumbers. It was time to put my plan into action. From here, I could cut straight across to the track without going near the shed, and turn right, up through the pass, unseen by the children, and in due course I could catch up with the rest of the refugee column, no doubt bedded down for the night a few miles further on.

What claim had Hannah and her children on me? They were not my kin; they were not even of my city. They belonged to Lachish, that unfriendly city which had so unfairly brought disaster on me and my father. As for the old man, no one could do much for him. The image of Rebecca, sitting by her fallen brother, stroking his hair and waiting trustingly for me to come back, rose up unbidden, and I pushed it from my mind. My father had told me to go home and look after my family.

My father. I stared down at burning Lashish. If only I *knew* what had happened to him. Here I am, Father, my mind called out. I'm thinking about you. Tell me what has happened to you.

The strange thing was that, however hard I pushed my thoughts at him, I could not conjure up his face in my mind's sight, nor catch his voice in my mind's hearing. A terrible desolation swept over me. If my father, whom I loved, could not only be taken from my life, but from my very memory, in less than a day, then my self-hood was a nothing, my soul was destroyed within me. The words that came into my mind were, of course, from the Psalms, for, as a well-brought-up son of a Temple servant, they were part and parcel of my deepest thoughts. That was something my father had said: when in trouble, repeat the Psalms. I began to gabble them over in my mind, psalm after psalm, like a spell to exorcise the demon of desolation, until I found my tongue repeating: 'Do justice to the afflicted and destitute. Rescue the poor and needy.'

I was pulled up short. I knew why I could not hear my father's voice, nor see his face. It was I who was hiding from him, I who was afraid to let him know what I was in the act of doing. What would my father think if he knew about Joel and Rebecca on the bare hillside? If he could see into the shed to which I was afraid to return? As for God seeing into my mind at this moment—a superstitious fear took hold of me that I would be responsible for my father's death if I ran away.

I started to walk steadily towards the shed, and all the time I walked, I heard my father's mild voice, and saw his face, as I had heard and seen him that morning, sitting on the wall in Lachish.

The old man lay dead across the entrance, his spade still grasped in his hand. It was too dark to tell what wounds he had, but a black pool lay beneath his breast. Nearby, a bundle of clothing lay on the ground. In it was wrapped the baby Reuben, his skull smashed. There was no sign of Hannah.

I felt no surprise, yet the reality shocked me. I could not grasp it. In a moment, everything would be as it was when we ate our meal round the home-made lamp; these images of death were no more than a passing fancy.

My hands knew what was to be done, although my brain kept on telling me this was all mere play-acting. I loosened the spade from the old man's grip, and dug a shallow trough by the edge of the cucumber field. Here I laid the baby, and covered it up as best I could with stones. Then I pulled the old man away from the doorway, but he was heavy, and his clothes dragged on the rough ground. I got him out of sight, round the side of the shed, and spread his blanket over him, holding it down at the corners with stones, to keep the vultures away. Then I set off back up the hill, wondering all the way what I was going to say to Joel and Rebecca.

They were sitting side by side where I had left them. When Joel saw that I was alone, he said, in the most matter-of-fact tones, 'My mother is dead, then, is she?'

'No,' I said. 'No. But they have taken her away with them.'

'They've most probably killed her by now, then,' he said, still in that flat, almost uninterested, tone of voice.

'Oh, I should think she will get away from them, in the dark. They were very drunk,' I said. It did actually make sense, but if it were true, why had she not returned?

'Is Reuben dead?'

'Yes.'

'And the old man?'

'Yes.'

After a pause, Joel asked, 'Are they dead in the hut?'

'No,' I said. 'I've buried Reuben, and the old man is round the back of the hut.'

'Will the men be coming back?'

'No, I'm sure not. Not tonight, anyway.'

Joel stood up. 'Let's go back to bed, then,' he said calmly. 'Come on, Becky.'

Rebecca had not said a word. I had no idea how much of the conversation she had taken in, and I was not going to try and find out. She simply held out a hand to each of us, and we walked back to the shed, lay down and went straight to sleep, as though nothing had happened. It was most peculiar.

I woke slowly, aware of the bright sun shining red through my closed eyelids. Some leaden feeling deep inside me warned me of formless horrors lurking just out of reach of memory. It was a dream, a bad and mercifully forgotten dream which I did not want to recall, but the sense of being in a strange place was too insistent to be ignored. I remembered where I was before I opened my eyes, and with that recollection came the train of events which had led to my being there. But the shadowy nameless thing that had happened since—ah, that, surely, was a dream? I felt around with my hand for Joel, and found him. Somewhere between us should be the old man's feet. I could not feel them, and I opened my eyes and saw Rebecca lying beyond Joel, as she had lain last night; but opposite us was nothing but the empty wall. It was true, then, was it? No dream? The shadow of a movement from the doorway made me sit up and swing round, heart pounding, and then blessed relief swept over me, for the figure sitting in the doorway was that of Hannah. She had her back to me, and was looking out. Of course; it was late; I had overslept. She would have the baby on her lap, and the old man would be out, perhaps looking for cucumbers.

She turned, and I saw her face, and knew it was no dream. A great raw bruise stood out against her white cheek and her eyes glittered through wet and matted hair. Her dress was torn and covered with mud, and she clasped one swollen ankle with a bleeding hand. But she was back, and despite everything, a great weight lifted from me.

I got up, and crawled out past her to sit in the cheerful sunshine.

'You got away,' I said.

'Yes.'

'I told Joel you would.'

'They are all right? They look all right.'

'Yes,' I said. Would she ask about Reuben, or did she know?

'It must have been you who buried Reuben,' she said.

'Yes,' I said. I did not know whether she was glad, or angry. 'I did not want the others to see him . . . like that.'

'It's all right,' she replied. 'He *was* dead. He must have been dead.'

I looked at her, startled. Of course he was dead. Half his small skull. . .

'I knew, at the time,' she said. 'I just had to be sure—he didn't regain consciousness.' I followed her glance and saw that the stones with which I had covered the shallow grave had been taken away; now smooth earth was patted carefully over it, and a single round stone was set in the centre.

'He didn't suffer,' she said. 'It happened so quickly.' She rubbed her swollen ankle, wincing a little. 'They killed the old man, I think. He tried to protect me. He hit one of them with the spade. If he had not done that, they might have left him alone.' She looked around. 'He must have crawled away somewhere.' She looked at the dark stain of blood on the earth.

'No,' I said. 'I dragged him round the back before fetching Joel and Rebecca.' I got up and walked round there; the humped blanket lay undisturbed where I had left it, but already flies were beginning to buzz around as the morning warmed up. 'I must bury him before we go,' I said, but as I spoke, my eye fell on her foot and I knew there could be little travelling that day.

'Don't you want to eat something first? Have they left the food?'

I had not thought about it, but when I went to look I found both our bundles still there, untouched, so that was one good thing. I decided I would rather start work before it got too hot, or more straying soldiers came our way, and would stop and eat when the children woke up. I walked over to the stream and drank from my cupped hands and then set to work.

Meanwhile, Hannah told me how she had managed to give the rioters the slip as they were approaching the army lines. Some other revellers had accosted them, and tried to snatch her from her captors, and in the drunken brawl that followed she had torn free from the one man left holding her, and run off across the fields. The men gave chase, but she would have got away easily enough had she not tripped over a rope tethering some sleeping camels, and fallen between the great beasts with a shooting pain in her leg. She lay crouched against one, daring neither to breathe nor moan, while the soldiers stumbled and grumbled and eventually took themselves off to their sleeping quarters. When at last she risked moving, she found she could not put any weight on the injured ankle. All night long she had crawled on hands and knees, back to the despoiled nest where she had left her young.

While I dug the old man's grave with his own good spade, I was thinking. There was no possibility of Hannah walking that day, or for several days, and by the time the children had woken, found their mother returned, and learnt all that they wanted to know about the night's events—which was not much, for the fact that she was back was enough—and we had sat down to eat together, I had worked out a plan. As soon as the old man was buried, I would slip quietly back down to Lachish, and see if I could find out what had happened, not only to my father, but also to Joash, the potter. They owned a donkey, Hannah told me, and maybe—just maybe—I would find it still tethered in their courtyard. Joash used it for carrying in the clay for his pots and sometimes to deliver the great earthenware jars, one wedged in each panier. She had not been allowed to bring the donkey out through the gate yesterday—it had been commandeered to carry boulders up to the catapult machines.

'But you will never be able to get out of Lachish with a donkey,' said Hannah. 'It will only draw attention to you; you'll get killed, or taken for a slave.'

I could not answer that. I had never been to a city the day after it had been taken by storm and I did not in the least know what to expect. There would be a lot of disorder and looting, but I supposed the Assyrians would not go on killing everybody in sight after the battle was over.

'I'll be careful,' I said.

Hannah sent the children to pick cucumbers while we buried the old man. When I had rolled the body into the rough hollow and filled it in with soil and stones, I laid the spade on top and covered it lightly with more earth. It was the nearest thing to family we could manage. We did not even know the old man's name, and when Hannah had fetched the children for the funeral prayers all I could call him was 'this old man'. This old man, and baby Reuben. I recited the service because I was the only man present—I had been initiated at the Temple a month earlier—and Hannah performed the ritual wailing, usually carried out by professional mourners, without their rhythmic clamour; but her mourning was from the heart.

'It's where he would wish to lie,' said Hannah, of the old man, when the ceremonies were accomplished; but she could not say the same for the small grave alongside.

Chapter 3

I felt excited rather than afraid as I walked back down the now-deserted track to Lachish. When I had fled, only the day before, I was a scared child, swept along mindlessly by the panicking throng. Now I was returning alone and by my own choice. I was a man, for I had taken decisions like a man, and bore a man's responsibility. Yesterday, with my father, even the thought of such burdens had overwhelmed me, but overnight, I had proved myself.

'How did you know you would find us here still?' I had asked Hannah, and she had replied:

'I did not expect to find *you* here; and without you, where else would the children have gone?' She was dividing out the meal cake at the time, and as I put my hand out for my share, she kept hold of the piece with me for a moment, saying. 'May the Lord bless and keep thee.'

Whether it was the effect of her prayer, I cannot say, but I felt strong and hopeful, despite the horrors of the last twenty-four hours, as I strode back to Lachish, even whistling as I went. From this distance, and under the bright sun, the Assyrians struck no terror. I was lithe and active, and knew that if I saw any approaching, I was far enough away to be able to outrun them.

The countryside ahead looked remarkably empty and although camp fires still sent up faint columns of smoke, everything was very quiet. A lark was singing somewhere above me, and a hoopoe strutted about, picking at some churned-up earth. A row of freshly cut stakes stuck up out of the ground nearby, and I realized with a shock of surprise that I was already in the area where camels had been picketed the night before—and they had gone. As I walked on, the ground became more and more churned up, and great black circles, some indeed still smoking, showed where bevies of men had been encamped; the young corn lay trampled into the dirt, fig and olive trees were browsed clean of leaves and twigs, the fists of pruned vines were kicked and broken where they thrust up out of the terraces in once-neat rows. Sennacherib's great army had gone as fast as it had come.

It seemed impossible; that was the secret of the Assyrians' success as invaders. Once embarked, they moved so fast from township to township that none were ready; the fleeing refugees from one city barely had time to spread panic in the next before the sound of the enemy battle-horns echoed in the ears of the watchman.

No soldiers had marched up the hill road to Hebron, however; they must have taken the more direct route north-west through Moreshat-Gath, and up the Elah valley. At this rate, they would reach Jerusalem before I could possibly get there by the safer but more circuitous road through Hebron. But at least, if they were gone, I would be able to find out about my father, and Joash; and even if the city were a place of destruction and death, I could see no reason why Hannah and her children should not return to it. It never occurred to me that the Assyrians would have left a garrison in the city, but I was only a boy, and knew nothing about the strategy of war.

Seeing the whole countryside around the Hill of Lachish shattered but empty, I walked boldly up to the side entrance through which I had fled so ignominiously the day before; boldly, but sickened by the tumbled heaps of corpses that lay all around me. At my approach, swarms of flies rose buzzing in the air, only to settle again upon the mangled bodies as I passed. They lay thickest on each side of the great ramp that the invaders had constructed, and which still blocked the main gateway. One broken battering ram lay on its side near the poles where the three corpses still hung; it had evidently slithered off the ramp, and the men who had been propelling it lay crushed within it.

Apart from the area of the parapet around the gatehouse tower on the outer wall, not much structural damage had been done to the lower defences. Once the Assyrians had taken the tower, they had used its shelter to launch their attack on the inner wall, bringing their own siege engines up the ramp, and using them to hurl rocks at the wooden doors beneath the inner gatehouse. Then, under protective cover from their bowmen, men had raced up the main roadway and set lighted faggots against the gates. Many died in the assault, but the gates burnt to ashes, and the army poured through.

All this I discovered later. Meanwhile, I walked in through the side gate and climbed the narrow stairs, only to find two tall Assyrian soldiers standing guard at the top. I stopped dead in my tracks, but one of them grabbed me by the scruff of the neck, and tossed me up the last few steps as though I were a puppy. As I stumbled and fell, the other soldier planted an ungentle foot on my belly and pinned me to the ground.

'Where've you sprung from, then?' demanded the first. He spoke a form of Assyrian I could understand easily enough, but I found I had nothing to say; my brain was turned to stone. I must have looked as I felt, a white-faced cowering child.

'Best take him to the Captain,' remarked the other and, removing his boot, he pulled me up by the hair and with one hand gripping my neck he steered me up the steep slope to the inner gate. So limp I felt with fear that my feet trailed behind me like a rag doll till the soldier gave me a kick on the shin and told me to walk on my own two feet.

He took me through the smoke-blackened gateway, where the remnants of the doors swung uselessly, into the square where yesterday the refugees had waited. Today, a tall officer was overseeing a detachment of soldiers who were herding a score of Lachish men into some sort of working party, each carrying a spade or pick. My guard pulled me along to the officer and reported the incident. The officer gave me a quick glance, and obviously found me neither interesting or useful, for he merely said, 'It's not important; let him go.' The soldier did just that, and I crumpled on the floor.

'Hop it,' said the soldier, and I fled.

But where could I flee to? The soldier probably assumed I lived in the city, and had a home, or the remains of a home, to go to. I ran blindly through the street till I came to the great central courtyard, and there I stopped and leaned against a wall, getting back my breath and my senses.

As the panic subsided, I began to see that nothing so very terrible had happened. I was inside the city, despite the armed guard on the gate, and I was free. I had achieved the very thing I had set out to do, and now I could set about looking for my father and Joash.

All I knew about Joash was that he was a small man and walked with a limp, having been trampled on by a horse when a child. His beard was not as dark as the hair on his head, but had a reddish tinge—like dried almond skin, said Joel. His donkey was called Bathsheba, after the beautiful mother of King Solomon.

Looking for my father came first, however, and I crossed to the storehouse where the doctors had been preparing to receive the wounded yesterday. I could hear the groans and cries of the wounded long before I entered, and when I got inside I saw the whole area was full of men, Assyrian and Judean, lying side by side. The same doctor whom I had seen yesterday was still there, bandaging an Assyrian soldier, his face lined with exhaustion, blood to his elbows. Nearby another doctor was stitching up a gashed forehead; he was new to me, and when he spoke to an orderly, it was in Assyrian. Soldiers stood guard at each end, and from time to time beckoned in a group of Lachish men under guard—slaves, really—to drag out another dead man.

I could not see my father, and I went cautiously up to the Judean doctor, keeping a wary eye on the soldiers, and asked about him. The doctor drew a weary hand across his forehead and said, yes, he remembered the Temple Officer; he had worked with him till nightfall, when he had gone out to look for the wounded, and had not returned. I was turning disconsolately away when the Assyrian doctor noticed me. 'Boy!' he shouted, 'fetch me some more water. We need more water.'

'Where from?' I asked.

'How do I know?' he snapped. 'You live here, don't you?'

I looked around for something to carry the water in, and the doctor nodded towards the wall where some great jars stood. As I picked one up, knowing I could not carry such a big jar on my head even empty—carrying waterpots is women's work, after all—and began to walk back the way I had come, one of the wounded men, a Judean, called me.

'The other way, son; the donkey's out there.' I looked where he pointed, and beyond the soldier on guard, by the arched doorway, I saw the rump of a donkey. When I got there, I found it was tethered ready, with two great empty panniers, one on each side.

'Bathsheba?' I said hopefully, but donkeys do not answer to their names like dogs. She just flicked her tail up and down and stared mournfully at the ground. I pushed the jar into one of the panniers and went back for another, pausing surreptitiously by the wounded Judean who had spoken to me before. Whatever happened, I did not want to draw attention to myself.

'Where's the well?' I muttered.

'It's been destroyed,' he said. 'You have to go down to the brook.'

'Outside the city?'

'That's right. You a stranger here?'

I nodded.

'Fine time for a visit.' He laughed, and winced with the

pain. I walked on to pick up the jar but as I came back past him he plucked my tunic.

'I know you,' he said. 'You were with that Temple Officer from Jerusalem.'

'He's my father. D'you know where I can find him?'

The man shook his head. 'He brought me in here—one of the last to make it. The Assyrians were already swarming over the city, and no more Judeans were to be brought to the hospital—those were their orders. Assyrians were to get the medical treatment—we could be cured more cheaply, with the sharp end of a spear.'

I looked around. Assyrians outnumbered Judeans, so far as I could see, but the two doctors appeared to be tending all men alike.

'Oh, in here it's different,' the man said, '—so far. Those two don't ask whether you serve Assur or Jehovah before anointing a man's wounds. I'm in no hurry to get out of here, I can tell you.'

'You still here? Hurry, boy!' The Assyrian doctor had seen me lingering.

'When did you last see my father?' I muttered.

'Last night, when he brought me in. He probably went back outside the walls.'

I could not stop to ask him what he meant, and I realized, as I untied the donkey and moved off, that I had not asked him how to get out of the city. The only way I knew was down the narrow staircase past the guards.

'Are you good at steps?' I asked the donkey, but she just plodded along as though she knew the way, so I let her take me. The only people about were Assyrians. The shops were empty and deserted, their shutters smashed and their goods looted. Only at the bakery was there any activity; here an armed soldier stood guard over the pale-faced baker and his assistants. There was no lack of customers for his loaves, but he would get no money for them; the invaders would devour them all.

Usually there would have been groups of men squatting on the street corners, women gliding erect beneath their water jars, and children playing games in the dusty thoroughfares, or grouped restlessly beneath the stern eye of a teacher. But the women and children had all fled, and the men were either dead or formed into slave gangs, to clear the aftermath of war and bury the dead. Now that I had a donkey and a job, I felt less conspicuous, but I began to be a little puzzled about the route the donkey was taking. She had begun by making her way downhill, but had then turned off and ambled along a series of winding alleys where the assault seemed to have made little impact. Suddenly she turned into a courtyard—a quiet place, with a fig tree casting a pleasant shade, rows of small earthenware jars glowing in the sun, and the gentle swish of a potter's wheel. There, plying his trade as if nothing had happened, sat a small man, with a round, serene face, and a beard the colour of dried almond skin.

'Joash?' I asked, hardly believing my luck.

He nodded. 'Brought my donkey back, have you?' he said. It was not luck, really. I had allowed the donkey her head, and she had used it to come home.

'I've come from Hannah,' I said. The wheel whirred to a stop, the rising mound of clay sinking back into a lump.

'Tell me,' said the potter. 'Go on.'

I began my story, and after a moment, because the wet clay was beginning to dry on the surface, he started the wheel up again, shaping and moistening the pot with absent-minded, practised hands. For a few seconds the spinning jar slowed as I told of the woman's scream, but the rhythm picked up again at once, and Joash kept it turning so until the thing was firm and dry enough to lift off.

In the silence that followed, I could not help thinking with compunction of those wounded men in need of water, and told Joash of my present task.

'Listen,' he said. 'I have a tank full of water, there, behind the kiln. It is for my work, but no one has thought of coming to take it. Fill your jars and take them up to the wounded; then come back and fill them a second time if they need it, for if they are short, it is our people who will go without. By then, I will have had time to think things out.'

The Assyrian doctor cursed me for being slow the first time I returned, but he must have wondered how I managed to make the second journey so quickly; if he had thought about it, that is, but his mind was on other things. My first two jars were empty again, so I loaded up Bathsheba once more and returned to the potter's yard.

There were two Assyrian soldiers there, shouting at Joash. They wanted big stone jars, like the ones he was making, but there were none ready baked. Fearful that they might commandeer not only my jars but Bathsheba as well, I backed the donkey softly out of the doorway and kept her padding on down the alley. I rounded a corner and found myself in a dead end, under the wall of the potter's yard. I could hear the soldiers shouting angrily, and some blows being struck, followed by the crash of breaking crockery. I waited till I heard the tramp of the soldiers' retreating feet, before cautiously returning to the yard.

I found Joash mopping at a weal on his cheek, and ruefully surveying the scattered pieces of all the small pots that had been neatly stacked against the wall.

'Fools!' he grumbled. 'Just because they couldn't have what they wanted.'

'Haven't you got any storage jars?' I asked.

'After yesterday? When every jar I had in stock was taken for oil, for firebrands, or for water for the wounded, and then smashed in battle? Why, I even saw the defenders hurling my jars at the enemy when they ran out of stones. My fine jars!' He ran his hand lovingly over the curve of a broken sherd. 'I reckon the only unbroken jars left in the whole city are the ones up at the storehouse, that you've been filling. And to smash these little phials, these flasks, and perfumery pots . . .' He waved disconsolately at the heap of rubble. 'Vandals, that's what these fellows are. Peasants!'

I looked at him wonderingly. The ordeal of his wife, the death of his baby son, had not seemed to move him as the destruction of his handiwork had done.

He looked up, aware of my silence. 'Does it surprise you to find me working in my yard, when all the rest of the world has gone mad?' he asked.

'A bit,' I said.

'Who have you seen selling goods today?' he asked.

'The baker,' I said.

'Oh, yes, today, the baker, to feed the men. Tomorrow, the miller, to keep the baker in grain. The day after, the potter, for how to store the bread and the grain, the oil and wine and water, the dried fruits and the salt and the pickled cucumbers? Eh?'

'I don't know,' I said. 'Anyway, those soldiers want your jars today.'

'That's because they are stupid. Anyone with any sense knows it takes three days at the least to make and fire a pot. I am allowed to work at my own trade today because there will be a demand for my pots as fast as I can have them ready.'

He was back at his wheel, moulding the ever-rising ring of clay.

'And yesterday?' I could not help asking, though I feared I might offend him. The only scar of battle he bore was the blow the soldier had just given him.

'Oh, yesterday,' he said with disgust. 'A mad day. Forced to lead my poor Bathsheba to and fro, to and fro, carting my precious jars up to the walls, to be destroyed. And at the end of it all, to have her taken from me by a gang of foreign louts!'

Bathsheba had taken herself over to the tank, and was having a long drink. Joash regarded her fondly. 'There's my beauty. I don't suppose any of those fools thought to water you since last night, eh?'

Time was passing. I wanted to go and look for my father. 'If I don't take this load back, I'll be in trouble,' I said.

Joash peered over at his tank, and grimaced when he saw the lowered level.

'That's the last you can take from here,' he said. 'And they'll have to find a new water-carrier after that, because I've worked out a plan, so listen.'

The plan had the merit of simplicity. I was to take Bathsheba out through the side entrance—yes, of course she could manage steps, said her master—on the pretext that I was fetching water for the wounded, and simply not return, but slip away, using whatever cover I could find, and take Bathsheba up to the cucumber field. Tomorrow, Hannah could ride to Hebron, and wait there till it was safe to return.

Remembering the events of the night, I realized it would be madness for Hannah to bring her children back into Lachish while it was still garrisoned. I had not seen a woman in the place, apart from an ancient dame working at the baker's and now that the main force had left by the Elah valley, Hebron looked likely to escape, for the time being at any rate. But if I could get out so easily, I asked, why not Joash? Why could he not come with us?

'And leave my home? My business?' Joash was quite shocked at the idea. 'These next few weeks will be a busy time for me,' he said, adding sadly, 'though I don't suppose the Assyrians will pay me for my pots. But if I go, they will destroy everything. Everything. Besides, I would not be allowed out of the gate. If I appear on the streets, some fool will most likely herd me off to dig graves like a slave.'

'What about me?' I asked.

'You are too small, and besides, you have a job already. You are the water-boy for the Assyrian doctor. Get him to give you a tablet with his written authority.'

'He thinks I've been out through the gate twice already,' I said. 'It'll seem a bit odd.'

'Pooh! Tell him they've changed the guard, and there's a new officer in charge, a bit of a stickler. Use your wits, lad.'

I certainly hoped they had changed the guard; my last encounter with them had not been encouraging.

'I'll give you some food to take back to Hannah,' Joash said.

'I can't take much; they'll see it.'

'I haven't got much,' he said. 'You're not very fat; we'll make you a little fatter.' He filled a couple of small bags with bread and dried fruit and a little flask of wine and another of oil and helped me to tie them round my waist under my tunic. As an afterthought he gave me an earthenware oil-lamp which had escaped destruction by soldiers.

I glanced back as I left the courtyard; the serene expression had returned to Joash's round face, as he pedalled at the wheel and shaped the glistening clay with skilful hands.

The doctor snorted scornfully when I spun my story about the written authority. He had no time for such nonsense, he said, and called to one of the soldiers and told him to accompany me down to the gate and tell the guard I was to be allowed through.

I was not too happy about this scheme, fearing that either the fact that I had not yet been through the gates with the donkey would emerge, or that the soldier would accompany me all the way to the waterhole. I was lucky, though; the guard *had* changed, and the soldier did not wait for me. All the same, I thought it advisable to fill my jars and come back, so that the guards would get used to me; next time perhaps they would not watch me so closely from the gateway.

I had reason to be glad they *did* watch me, for another soldier, in charge of a grave-digging party, would have commandeered Bathsheba despite my protestations if the guard had not shouted to him that I was to be allowed to continue with my task. I was relieved to see three women walking up towards me with their pitchers on their heads, for it showed me where to go; they were young, I noticed with surprise as they passed me, finely dressed and with rouged cheeks and darkened eyes and they spoke to each other in the dialect of the Philistines. Philistia, I knew, had been conquered some twelve years earlier; most likely these women were camp-followers, come to terms with their Assyrian lords. It was no doubt in Ashkelon, not far away on the coast of the Great Sea, that the Assyrian host had foregathered before making the assault on Lachish.

Taking Bathsheba down the steps with her empty jars had been quite easy; getting her back up when they were full of water was as hard work for me as for her; I had to get behind her and heave with all my might, while the guards watched me and laughed. However, when I came down the second time, one of them—quite a friendly young man, to my astonishment—told me that the east gate was now open, and it would be a much easier way for me to get back into the city, as there were no steps. This was a great piece of luck, as it meant nobody would notice my non-return.

After I had followed the track towards the stream for a short distance, I glanced back and made sure the guards were not watching me this time. There was no sign of them, so I cut quickly round to the right, where the remains of the ramp soon hid me from their view. There was a lot of activity all around me, for the ramp was being dismantled by a team of captives—mixed, so far as I could see, with a few wretched-looking slaves, the survivors of those who the previous day had built that very ramp at such cost in human lives. Another gang—all Lachish men—were still clearing away the corpses; each was inspected by an Assyrian officer, and if they were Assyrian dead, they were laid out in a row, ready for honourable burial conducted by the priests of Assur later in the day. The Judaean dead were thrown without ceremony into a mass grave some way from the city walls. Was my father among them? When I first came to the city that morning, it had not occurred to me that my father's body could be one of those among which I had picked my way, but now I stared fearfully at every poor corpse, especially those whose robes were whiter and finer than ordinary. Finally, I steeled myself to walk over to the mass grave, and peer in. One glance was enough. There was no hope of recognizing anyone in that mound of tangled and mutilated bodies, and I turned quickly away, sickened by the mud and blood, the flies and the stench. A huge Assyrian towered over me, his mouth red and gaping in a cruel grin above the curled beard.

'Looking for someone?' he said. 'Go on. Take a closer look,' and he made as if to push me into that awesome pit. I dodged and ran, pursued by his mocking laughter, dragging Bathsheba after me.

I would now have to walk right round the back of the Hill of Lachish in order to have any chance of making my getaway unseen, and I reckoned my safest course was to keep close beneath the wall, and just hope no guards were posted above me. The other danger was that one of the soldiers in charge of the slave gangs would see fit to question my movements. I walked steadily away without looking back, but all the time I feared a shout from behind, and cudgelled my brains to think of some good reason for taking a donkey laden with empty water pots round the back of the city walls.

Certainly, nobody else had any business there. I soon found myself alone, scrambling along at an awkward angle round an ever-steepening slope. It was not surprising that there was no gate, and few defensive towers, on this side, for the lie of the land made the walls impregnable. Bathsheba objected to having to follow such a difficult route when it was obvious to her that by dropping down the slope she could get her four feet on much more level ground, and we proceeded crabwise in a state of increasing mutual irritation. A rocky outcrop jutted from the slope ahead of us and I was as anxious to keep Bathsheba above it as she was determined to get on to the goat track that ran below it. If she had not leaned so heavily against me that I was forced to veer off-course, I would have passed Adad and my father without noticing them.

It was the glimpse of white that caught my eye first, the white of the fine Temple cloth; when I got closer I saw the dark stains of dried blood; and the scarred brown limbs and purple on the tunic of the man who crouched beside the still body.

I was puzzled that the huddled figure appeared neither to hear nor see our approach but as I drew nearer, my bare feet and Bathsheba's soft hooves padding quietly on the turf, I could hear him moaning; and when, eventually, he did turn his face towards us, I saw that he was blinded.

I had no sense of shock or surprise when I recognized the dead body cradled in the Assyrian's arms as that of my father. I somehow knew it, from the moment I saw the white robe in the shadow of the rock. Strangely, my first emotion was not one of grief, but of immense happiness—and yet I broke down in uncontrollable weeping. Two thoughts only filled my mind; that my father's body was in my safe keeping, and not tumbled in that dire pit of death, nameless and forsaken; and that I was no longer alone. It was because of the happiness that the tears flowed, like an icicle melting.

Something must have told me that the blinded soldier posed no threat, for I took no more notice of him than if he had been a harmless dog, but gathered my father into my arms, sharing him with this stranger who held the dead man so tenderly. Gradually, though, I became aware of his hands touching me, cautiously.

'What is it? What is it?' he kept saying, in his foreign dialect. I turned my head and looked at him through blurred eyes. A terrible inflamed weal ran right across one side of his face and blood-encrusted hair stuck to the place where his eye should have been. His other eye was closed beneath a great wound which, unexpectedly, had been cleaned and roughly stitched up, although the rest of his face, hands and bare legs were ingrained with dirt and blood. I turned my eyes away from the terrible face to the hand that lay on my forearm; it was scarcely bigger than my own hand, slight, and supple; the hand of a boy. I looked him up and down, and realized he was a youth scarcely older than myself, the only difference being that whereas I was just too young to fight, he was just too old to be left behind when the Assyrian war-machines set forth.

'What is it?' he said again. It was not really a question, for he kept repeating the words tonelessly, like something learnt by rote whose meaning has long since been forgotten.

'This man,' I said, 'this man is my father. I have been looking for him, and now I have found him.'

I gazed down at my father's face. It was unmarked and perfectly calm, and I felt his friendly, reassuring presence as fully as if his spirit still lived behind those cold closed eyelids; but the boy, with his ravaged visage and monotonous moan, was as remote to me as a piece of carrion. His next words, though, pierced my indifference.

'You must kill me,' he said. 'Only I have no sword. Have you a sword?'

'No,' I said.

'Nor has he,' said the boy, running his fingers down my father's arm to his hand; he opened the limply-clenched fist, and a little trickle of dust ran out. He must have clutched the earth in his last brief agony of death. Why had he died here, in this empty place, and why was his enemy cradling him so gently? 'He was a healer,' the boy went on. 'He had no use for a sword.'

'He was my father,' I said again. 'A Judaean.' He did not seem to have taken in that I was of the enemy race, even though he had asked me to kill him.

'He found me here, and stitched up my wound,' he put his hand up to the joined edges of the cut across his brow, 'and bathed it with some wine he had with him. He said in a little while he would try and fetch water to wash this—,' he sketched a gesture towards the other, torn, side of his face, 'but he must rest because he had been injured. So we stayed here all night and he talked to me when the pain was bad; but as time went on, his breathing got very weak, and he left off talking. Then, after a long time, he said, "It is sunrise," but it was still all dark to me. I held him, like this, to help him keep breathing, but it was no good. It just stopped.'

'That was a long time ago,' I said. 'Why do you still sit here, holding him?'

'What else can I do?' he said. 'While he breathed, it was not so dark.'

'You could find your way back to the city,' I said. 'You must know your people have taken it.'

'No, no, they would kill me. Stone me, or beat me to death or—like those Jewish spies.'

'No,' I said, for I thought he had not understood. 'It is the Assyrians—your people—who are in command now. Our people would not dare kill you.'

'I know that,' he said. 'But with our people it is the rule. It is always what happens to deserters. Otherwise, too many men would run away.'

Up till then, I was only interested in getting him to talk so that I could learn more about my father's last hours, but his latest words startled me. I had never thought of Assyrians not *wanting* to fight.

'You ran away?' I said.

He paused a long while, staring down some unseen corridor of horror, while the flies buzzed and settled on his bleeding face, and his hands lay slack on my father's body. 'My own people will kill me if I go back,' he said, 'and your people will kill me if I do not; or I will die here of thirst and poison from my wounds; and when I am dead, Assur will torment me for ever because I ran away and did not fight for him.'

I thought how while I had been enduring a night of savagery, this boy had been foremost in my dying father's care, and in a sudden burst of anger I said, 'You're in a bad way, aren't you?'

His wretchedness was far too deep for my childish envy to hurt, but my words caught his attention. 'That's what your father said,' he murmured.

What had I said? 'You're in a bad way, aren't you?' The words echoed in my mind, but in a very different tone from the one I had used. How often, with just that phrase, had my father gathered me up, a roaring toddler with grazed knees, or a few years older, angry and hurt by some seemingly unjust scolding from one of my other relations, and by his manner of saying it, instantly rubbed out the injury to a point of total insignificance.

'I'm sorry,' I muttered, more to the dead man than the living one. As I looked down once more at my father's face, I knew he had left me a legacy I could not refuse.

'Listen,' I said. 'I'll help you if you will help me.'

'There's nothing to be done,' he said, hopelessly.

'Yes, there is,' I said. 'I must bury my father with all the proper prayers and ceremonies for our God, Jehovah.'

'Of course,' he said. 'I will pray to Shamash for him, and to Ea and Ishtar, but not to Assur, for Assur is angry with me and it would not help him.'

'Don't bother,' I said. 'Your gods are trash. Anyway,' I went on quickly, because I had spoken without thinking and the last thing I wanted was to start a theological argument, 'I have a donkey here, and I want to get my father's body on to the donkey and take it up the valley to where I have friends, well away from your army, where I can bury him in peace. You must help me lift him.'

'Have you any water?' he asked.

'No, but I have wine.' I had the small bundles of food and flask of wine which Joash had given me, but I had not troubled to fill the water pots because I could do that in the stream by the cucumber field. I fetched the flask and held it to his lips while he gulped some down. I gave him a piece of bread, too, but he only took one mouthful and though he chewed he did not seem able to swallow it. However, the wine revived him a little, and he seemed willing enough, in a docile manner, to try and do what I asked, even before I had explained the rest of my plan.

This was that, having loaded the body on to Bathsheba, I should take the Assyrian with me up the valley, for as soon as I had rounded the back of the fortifications and struck off up the pathway to Hebron, I would be almost bound to be spotted by sentries, or meet some work party. If I could appear to be under orders from an Assyrian soldier in full uniform, I would be less likely to be challenged; the only question was whether the blind youth was strong enough, or spirited enough, to make the journey. 'And afterwards,' I said, to encourage him, 'maybe I can find someone who will look after you.' Who, I could not imagine, but he just nodded, and said, 'I will try, because he was my friend.'

This time, I checked the jealous retort.

I had noted earlier, because it stuck in my subconscious mind as odd, my father's legs, long and pale, sticking out from his Temple robe, but it was only as we came to move him that I realized a handsbreadth or more had been torn neatly from the whole circumference. Then I saw a narrow strip, like a bandage, lying on the ground. The Temple Steward had gone to his death looking like a slave or herdsman in a short tunic because he had been tearing his robe, strip by strip, to bind up the wounded of both camps. I guessed what the last strip had been intended for, but I pocketed it without saying anything to my companion. From the back, and at a distance, which is how I expected us to be seen, he would look more like an ordinary soldier without a white bandage round his head.

My father's body was too long to lie athwart the little donkey, but we managed with some difficulty to wedge him lengthways between the empty waterpots so that his arms fell each side of the animal's neck. Bathsheba accepted the heavy load resignedly—she had spent her time off pulling hungrily at the tough clumps of rock roses and no doubt felt revived—and so we started on the long slow trek towards the head of the valley, with good news for Hannah's family, but for me, another grave to dig.

Chapter 4

At first, I took Bathsheba's halter and told the Assyrian to walk on the other side, holding on to the pannier for guidance, but he stumbled and whimpered so, and made our progress so slow, that I was forced to walk on the further side of him to guide his steps over the rough ground. It is difficult to walk holding somebody's hand and feel nothing for them, yet that was what I tried to do. All my instincts forbade me to feel kindness, but piety for my dead father prohibited me from being cruel. So we went on, he despairing of consolation, and I withholding it.

Although nervous about the possibility of encountering foraging parties on our way up the valley, I had expected it to be, in general, as deserted as when I had come down that morning. I was therefore astonished, as we rounded the slope and prepared to work diagonally away from the city towards the Hebron road, to look down on a scene of teeming activity. Where, that morning, only blackened circles of ash and a few ragged picket stumps had marked the overnight stands of the army, now there were crowds of shouting men, and camels laden with baggage, and great carts drawn by bullocks. A huge tent lay spread-eagled on the ground, surrounded by men pulling on ropes or hammering stakes into the ground. As I watched, the whole structure rose from the ground on four sturdy poles, hauled up by chained gangs of slaves and fastened to the prepared pegs. Immediately workmen ran forward and fixed the flapping side in place and even before this was done, a great purple carpet was being heaved out of a bullock cart and carried inside. Wall hangings, carved tables and other ornate pieces of furniture were unloaded and carried in, and from another bullock cart six men lifted down a vast golden throne.

'It is the Royal Pavilion,' said the blind boy, when I described the scene to him. 'Sennacherib is setting up his headquarters here.'

'Here?' I said. 'I thought he was marching on Jerusalem.'

'No. My . . . his Commander-in-chief, the Rabshakeh, goes to Jerusalem with the King's terms of surrender. The King is to stay here, with the main army.'

'But most of the troops who were here yesterday have gone.'

'Oh, yes. They have other settlements to capture. But the King has a large force with him, too. When they have taken Gath, they will leave a garrison there, as they have in Lachish, but the rest will join the King here, to wait for your King's surrender.'

'How do you know all this?' I asked. It struck me, not only that he was remarkably knowledgeable for a raw recruit, but also that I could understand his Assyrian much more easily than that of most of the enemy I had encountered—he spoke more like the doctor.

He did not answer and I was about to repeat the question when I noticed that two of the soldiers were looking up at us curiously, and I realized I must make up my mind quickly what to do. In fact I had little choice, because to turn round and go back would look suspicious, so I urged Bathsheba steadily forward, aiming to give the throng as wide a berth as possible. The two men began to walk along the road as if to meet us, and my heart started to thump uncomfortably. The men appeared puzzled rather than hostile, but I could think of no plausible reason why I should be escorting a blind Assyrian and a dead Judaean on a stolen donkey up the Hebron road.

Bearing in mind that my companion was as afraid of his

countrymen as I was, I explained the situation to him. 'Are they officers, or rankers?' he asked.

'I don't know. How can you tell?'

'What have they on their feet?'

'Sandals.'

'Shin shields? Helmets?'

'Yes; but their tunics are plain, with no ornamented bands, and they have nothing on their wrists.' As I spoke, I glanced at the boy's own arms, each with its gold-tooled leather guard, and a wide gold bracelet above the elbow.

'What sort of age?'

'One's quite old; his beard is greyish; the other—a bit younger, I think.'

The boy nodded. 'Leave it to me,' he said. 'You must act like my servant; and if you have to speak, call me the Lord Adad. They are probably only sergeants.'

'Is Adad your real name?'

'Yes.' He paused, as though sensing he had made a mistake, and then added, 'No matter; it is a common enough name.'

The older man shouted to Adad as we approached, asking if he needed help, and Adad called back that he had to go up the mountain with a sacrifice to appease Shamash, and make an image to trap the demon who had taken away the sight of his eyes.

This sounded like rubbish to me, for with facial wounds like Adad's, he scarcely needed to blame a demon for his blindness, but the men seemed to accept the story, and only asked whether he would like a soldier to accompany us, in case 'the slave-boy' took advantage of the master's blindness to run off.

'Shamash says I must go alone,' said Adad. 'Besides, the boy's family are held hostage for him.'

The men saluted and left us to go on our way, though I had a notion, which I did not dare to put to the test by turning round, that they stood watching us for a long time.

Adad, I realized, was shaking violently, but whether

from fear, or pain and exhaustion, I did not know. The incident had drawn us together, and after a while I asked him why he trembled so.

'It is terrible to die as a deserter,' he said. 'And those men—if they were of Sennacherib's own guards, they might have recognized me.'

'If they have only just arrived, they would not have known you were a deserter,' I said.

'Not at once, perhaps; but sooner or later it would be discovered; and my father. . .'

His voice died away. 'Is your father an officer in the King's forces?' I prompted him. He hesitated a moment, and then said, with a mixture of pride and despair, 'My father is the Rabshakeh.'

I stared at him, disbelieving at first, but as I turned his words over in my mind, I could think of no reason why he should invent such a claim. 'The Rabshakeh,' I knew, was the title given to the Commander-in-Chief of the army; he it was who had demanded the surrender of Lachish, and who had now been dispatched to carry the King's terms to Jerusalem. In normal circumstances, his son would be a most valuable hostage to fall into the hands of the Judaeans, and it would only make sense for Adad to admit his identity if he was clutching at a chance to save his own skin. But when he could have been rescued by the Assyrian sergeants just now, he had plainly been as terrified of being challenged by them as I was. Besides, observing his whole demeanor of abject despair, his fearful injuries and pain, I could not believe that he was capable of deliberate deception.

But would his commanding officer dare to impose such a shameful death penalty as Adad had spoken of, upon the son of the Commander-in-Chief, now, while the Rabshakeh himself was on his way to Jerusalem as an emissary from one king to another? Would he, perhaps, have been kept prisoner until his father returned? Or would the whole episode be hushed up, and everyone pretend it had never happened? I thought about the Assyrian reputation as brave and pitiless warriors, and I came to the conclusion that Adad's behaviour forcibly confirmed the truth of his story—except for one thing.

'I do not believe the son of the Rabshakeh would run away in battle,' I said, watching the blind face, the face that could not watch me back.

He made no answer, except to shake his head slightly, but his lip trembled, and he pressed the back of his hand to his mouth. When, a little later, I tried again, saying, 'Why did you run away? What happened?' I got no response at all. I do not think he heard me.

Because he was in soldier's uniform, and taller than me, and an enemy, I do not think I realized just how hard I was driving him. By the time we reached the shed, he was far, far away in a private hell of his own which required him to put one foot in front of another, in darkness and pain, for ever and ever. I prised open the fingers that clutched the donkey's pannier, and he crumpled in a heap on the ground.

I had expected Hannah and the children to come out to meet me when they saw me returning with Bathsheba, but all was silent, and when I looked inside the shed, it was deserted. Even our few pieces of baggage had gone; apart from the new graves and the dark stain in the dust by the doorway, the place might have been unvisited for months.

The angry thought crossed my mind that Hannah had taken her children and gone to Hebron, leaving me to my fate but then I remembered her sprained ankle. She could not have gone far, unless they had been carried away by the Assyrians. I looked all round, and it was then that I saw the dark head of Joel, peeping out from the gully. I waved at him, and the head disappeared momentarily, and then Joel popped up again and beckoned to me. I hesitated a moment, casting an anxious glance at Bathsheba, standing patiently under the heavy weight of my father, and then ran across, fearing some disaster. But no, they were all three crouched in the stream bed, apparently unharmed.

'Who is he? What does he want?' whispered Hannah. It was then I realized what had put them to flight—the distant sight of me toiling up the road apparently under the guard of an Assyrian soldier. I reassured them there was no danger, and as they followed me dubiously back, I outlined the main events of the day. The children stood at a safe distance from the huddled Adad, staring at him with a kind of horrified fascination, while Hannah limped over and helped me take off the pannier and slide my father's body to the ground.

For Joel and Rebecca, the fact that my father was dead meant little compared to the news that their father was alive and well; and as soon as they could tear themselves away from the sight of the wounded Assyrian soldier, they came up to pet Bathsheba, and lead her down to the stream for a drink and a chance to feed on the lusher vegetation that grew there.

'There's bread, and figs, and some oil and wine in the water jars,' I said carefully. 'Joash sent them. The oil is in the little jar, and the wine . . .' Why was I repeating these things as though they were important? Hannah would find them all anyway. But I went on, as I stood staring down at the corpse of my father, thinking of the trickle of dust in his hand. The dust kept trickling on and on till it was heaped up in a great mound, like a grave, shutting me off from him for ever; there was a grave to be dug, another one, and I must dig it.

'The figs,' I said, 'are wrapped up in five big leaves—or maybe four . . .'

Hannah put her arm round me. 'I'll find them,' she said. 'You sit down here, and drink this.' She held the wine flask to my lips. 'Can you eat anything?' I shook my head; the world suddenly seemed very far away. 'Then sleep.'

I made a last effort to remember what I ought to be doing. 'My father . . .' I began.

'I will watch by your father,' she said, 'and that poor boy.' Her last remark made no sense to me, for I had forgotten about Adad. I knew there was something I was trying to say about my father, but it all seemed too difficult, and I sank into sleep. Through my dreams, however, I was troubled by the recurring image of my father's two thin, pale legs sticking out from the shortened robe. I knew I must cover them up, but I could not find any way of doing it.

When I awoke, it was quite dark. Adad was moaning nearby, but it was, I think, Joel's piercing whisper that had roused me. 'Tell him to be *quiet*,' he was saying, his voice made querulous by fear. Someone must have carried or led me into the shed, though I had no recollection of it happening. Joel's voice came from my left, and on my right I could feel the Assyrian turning restlessly. From beyond him, apparently from outside the doorway, came the calm voice of Hannah: 'It's all right; there is no one to hear him.'

'But there *might* be,' said Joel. 'Soldiers might come, like last night.'

'If they do, I shall see them in time.'

'If we have to run, you'll come with us this time?'

'Yes.'

'What happens if you fall asleep?'

'I shall not fall asleep. You are quite safe.'

I dozed off again, and slept till broad daylight.

I woke this time to the sound of children's laughter. The sun was streaming in, and across the bright square of light a succession of dancing silhouettes flitted by. Joel and Rebecca were chasing each other round and round the shed, as merrily as though the events of the last two days had never been. I clambered out just in time to see Joel, intent on his game of catch, leaping across the blanketed body of my father as though it were no more than a handy log. Rebecca tried to stretch and touch him, but stumbled and fell over the obstacle. At once both children fell silent, and when Joel saw me standing there, he seized Rebecca by the hand and ran off, saying, 'Come and play over here; there's more room.'

I looked around for Hannah, but it was Adad I saw first.

He was sitting propped against a rock, facing full into the sun, his wounds bathed and cleaned, his eyes bandaged with the soft white cloth I knew so well. Below the bandage, the lines of anguish showed less deep, and his mouth drooped in the natural relaxation of repose. Whether he was really asleep, I could not tell, but Hannah certainly was. Her light but persistent snoring drew my attention to where she lay, awkwardly huddled, having dropped off in the act of tidying away the remains of the morning meal. No doubt she had watched all night, and slept little since the dawn of the attack on Lachish. I took the bread from her hand, laid her carefully down in a more comfortable position, and fell upon the bread ravenously.

Adad tilted his face, as if to listen. 'Who is that?' he asked. 'Is it the son of the healer?'

'Yes,' I said. 'It is Benjamin. I've only just woken up.'

'I slept a little, too. Why did you not kill me when I was asleep?'

'I did not think about it,' I said, chewing bread hungrily. 'Besides, I have no weapon, and I was too tired.'

He turned his head away, back to face the warmth of the sun. 'Your mother is kind, like your father,' he said, 'but you, I think, are a child.'

'You did not ask me to be kind; you asked me to kill you,' I retorted. 'Anyway, Hannah is not my mother. We are all just refugees escaping from Lachish, and I do not know why she has looked after you. Your soldiers have killed her baby and would have taken her away for their pleasure, but she escaped from them in the dark.'

He sighed deeply. 'It is all dark for me,' he said. 'I hate war.'

'Is that why you ran away?'

He was silent for a long time and I thought he was not going to answer, but then he said. 'No, I ran away because I was afraid.' After another pause, he went on, haltingly, 'You do not know what it is like. Up under the walls, with arrows flying everywhere, and those flaming brands, and men all around screaming, and dying; and the slaves being driven to slaughter like cattle; and I, who want to be an architect and build great cities, standing there with nothing to do but destroy and be destroyed and all for the glory of Sennacherib. Battle after battle, I stand there, doing what I hate, because I am the Rabshakeh's son; hoping the others do not see I have wetted myself in my fear, and for nothing, but to inflict pain and fear on other people. Each time, I say, maybe this is the last; maybe Sennacherib will have had enough, and go home; maybe I will get killed, and the fear will cease with everything else; but always there is another battle.'

'Is that why you decided to run away?'

'Decided? No, there is no decision. Suddenly, a shower of brands comes down, and one strikes me here'—he put his hand to his right eye—'and the rag on it sticks to me, burning, and I tear it away, and I am running, running, anywhere to get away from the pain, away from the fighting. There is a huge officer in front of me, crying, "Back! Back!" and waving his sword, but I take no notice, and run straight at him, as though to run into his arms for safety. And he takes his sword, and strikes me clean across the face, here'—and he put his hand to his left temple—'and I run on, on, but can see nothing. I fall, and get up again, and keep on running, many times, till I reach ground so steep that when I fall, I roll over and over, down a great slope; and all is quiet, and dark, and the fighting is far away, but the pain is still with me, more than I can bear.'

'Is that when my father found you?'

'Not then, but later. I do not know how much later. Hours. Sometimes I think a lifetime. How can I tell? Day, night, unless I can feel the sun on my face, what can I tell of time?' He stretched out his arms, feeling about him. 'I cannot even be sure it is the sun. Blind, among enemies, the warmth I feel could be a burning brand held before me, ready to be dashed into my face.'

I took his hands then, and held them in my own. While he was speaking, the picture had come unbidden to my mind of myself in that fleeing mob, trampling panic-stricken over the dead and dying. Were we not both runaways? Whatever the Assyrian army meant to me, this boy was no enemy. Dragged on an orgy of slaughter for five hundred miles, to be left blinded and disgraced in an enemy land, he was as much a victim of the war as any of us.

I said, 'I must go now and dig a grave for my father. I am glad you were with him, that he was not alone when he died.' And I went to retrieve the spade from under its light covering of earth on the old man's grave.

After I had been digging for a while, Adad called to me and asked where the grave was, and whether he could help. I gave him the spade while I rested, but I could see he was not able to make much of a job of it, and the exertion plainly set his head throbbing. While he tried, I told him who we were, and what had happened since we had left Lachish, and how we would be making our way to Hebron as soon as possible.

'What will you do with me, then?' he asked.

It was the question that was bothering me, and I did not know how to answer it. 'Ask Hannah,' I said.

'I've not gone to all that trouble cleaning his wounds and binding him up to leave him here to die, or be murdered,' she said. 'He must come with us, but not in that uniform, not if we're going to Hebron.' She had woken, and was setting out the ritual offerings for the funeral. She was worried that we had no live animal to slaughter, to pour out the warm blood upon the rough stone altar, but I was glad. If there was one thing above all else in which my father resembled my grandfather Isaiah, it was in his disapproval of the people's obsession with sacrifices. He had taught me a passage from one of my grandfather's teaching poems and, when later that day, I stood by the graveside, I repeated it as well as I could remember it:

> '"Your countless sacrifices, what are they to me?" says the Lord;

"I am sated with whole-offerings of rams
and the fat of buffaloes;
I have no desire for the blood of bulls,
of sheep and of he-goats.
Whenever you come to enter my presence
who asked you for this?
No more shall you trample my courts.
The offer of your gifts is useless,
the reek of sacrifice is abhorrent to me.

"When you lift your hands outspread in prayer,
I will hide my eyes from you.
Though you offer countless prayers,
I will not listen.
There is blood on your hands;
wash yourselves and be clean.
Put away the evil of your deeds,
away out of my sight.
Cease to do evil and learn to do right,
pursue justice and champion the oppressed;
give the orphan his rights, plead the widow's cause."'

I paused, and glanced round wondering how long I should go on for. Rebecca was getting restive, though Joel stood obediently, already trained to listen to long readings from the Holy Scrolls at school. Hannah was watching me with a slightly puzzled look on her face, for these were not the verses I had duly recited over the old man and the infant whom we had buried yesterday. Adad stood a little apart, his hands outstretched to the sun which he could feel but not see, his lips moving silently. I wondered what strange gods he was invoking, and whether he was praying for my father or for himself.

Adad had mentioned that he had never wanted to be a soldier, but an architect; and I was destined to be brought up in the priestly tradition. We were both just sacrifices, like the bullocks and the he-goats offered up by Sennacherib's army to placate the Assyrian gods and give them a bigger bit of land to rule over. Our people used to think that way about Jehovah, as though he were an ordinary war-lord who could only extend his territory by sending troops to kill and burn in all the neighbouring lands; but my grandfather said that was all wrong. The Assyrians themselves were no more than tools used by Jehovah to teach our people more about his true nature. But then, that would mean our God was harsh, and *did* demand bloody sacrifices—like the death of a brave old man, an innocent baby, and my own gentle father.

I had paused so long while these thoughts chased through my mind that the others were beginning to wonder if I had finished. Some verses from further on in the passage came into my mind, which seemed to contradict the bleak direction in which my thoughts had led me, and I repeated them with a growing conviction:

'For instruction issues from Zion,
and out of Jerusalem comes the word of the Lord;
he will be judge between the nations,
arbiter among many peoples.
They shall beat their swords into spades,
and their spears into pruning-hooks;
nation shall not lift sword against nation,
nor ever again be trained to war.'

Adad had asked me if I had a sword, to kill him with; but I had only a spade, and I used it now, to shovel the earth into my father's grave, covering his naked legs.

Chapter 5

Later that afternoon, I exchanged clothes with Adad, and walked back down the valley in the hope of seeing the Assyrian King, Sennacherib.

Looking back now, and thinking about all I had been through in the past three days, and my grief at the death of my father, and the deep and sombre emotions which took possession of me during the burial ceremony, it seems extraordinary to me that the very same day I should have wanted to indulge in a dangerous and boyish prank.

Maybe it was not so very surprising. I was just coming up to my thirteenth birthday, a normally energetic and lively boy who had suddenly been called upon to act like a man, make decisions like a man, and face disaster like a man; but boyhood is not dead and buried in three days. When it was decided to wait until the morning to make the trip to Hebron, to avoid having to spend a night on the way, and to give both Hannah and Adad a little longer to recover from their injuries, I found myself with half a day in which to do what I liked. Hannah was tired, the children were growing peevish, and I could not bear to sit around with nothing to do but brood upon my father's death, the sad spectacle of Adad always before me. I said I would see if I could get hold of a peasant's rough dress for Adad, and meanwhile we should exchange my schoolboy tunic for his soldier's gear so that I could pass unheeded down the valley.

Hannah did not want me to go, but when Joel began to nag that he wanted to come with me, she was glad to see me make off with all speed, and so put an end to Joel's pleading.

The leather tunic was rather too long, and felt strange and heavy on me, as did the shin shields and wrist bands. Adad said that if I wore these, people would take me for an officer cadet like himself, and be less inclined to question me than if I were a common boy soldier. He was unwilling to let me wear the broad gold bracelets that encircled his upper arms, but I insisted upon taking them. He had, of course, lost sword, helmet and leather shield in his flight.

As I came into full view of the valley I paused, astounded at the change that had taken place yet again. Now it was crammed with people; they filled the plain like the sea, lapping at the hillside and encircling the mound on which Lachish stood as though it were an island. This was not like the army that had marched into the attack two days before, for now Lachish itself appeared no longer to be the focus of attention. This swarming mass of men was busy creating its own city of tents, with its own thoroughfare, stables, and workshops; the broken battlements of Lachish were no more than an unregarded backdrop to a foreign settlement that covered an area much greater than the huddle of dwellings on the hill.

The only clear space was around the Royal Pavilion, which I had seen being erected the day before. Some sort of fence—I could not see from this distance whether it was of poles or of soldiers, but there was a glint of metal that suggested spears—enclosed this open space, and from it a number of clearly-defined thoroughfares radiated outwards, the area between each filled with an orderly, close-packed arrangement of tents, fire-trenches and animal lines. It was hard to believe this teeming city, for so it struck me, occupied a space that until a couple of days ago had been fields of corn, and groves of figs and olives. A few trees still stood, but many had been hacked down to provide firewood, ancient trees each of which, no doubt, was the prized possession of one family who had depended upon its harvest for generations to keep them supplied with oil and dried fruits.

I began to regret my scheme of changing with Adad. As a Judaean boy I might have hung cautiously around the outskirts, able to trust to my legs and the shelter of the hills if anyone challenged me, and after all, I had got along all right yesterday without disguise. As an Assyrian soldier, I would only draw attention to myself if I skulked around on the periphery, but the thought of marching boldly into the centre of the Assyrian encampment now appeared nothing short of madness.

I could, of course, turn round and walk back, and say I had changed my mind. . . .

I looked down at my military uniform, straightened my shoulders and my resolve, and marched steadily on.

The Hebron road ran along the edge of the valley, so there was little room for any troops to camp between it and the hills on that side; it was all on my right that the great host was busy settling itself, and I was able to stroll along unnoticed past a number of alleys running down at right-angles from the road, dividing the encampment into sections. It struck me that each section housed a particular battalion, each with its own commanders and its own system; the uniform varied from section to section, and so, too, did the dialects in which the men spoke to each other. One battalion spoke a language I could barely understand, and the men for the most part had crisp, brownish hair and ruddy complexions; some had skin as pale as ivory, and others were as dark as old leather. Some were of a type familiar to me, for they were our old neighbours and enemies, the Philistines, from the coastal strip not far from Lachish. Sargon, Sennacherib's father, had taken Ashdod, Philistia's chief city, in the year I was born, and it had been a vassal state ever since. How much the Philistines relished having to fight Sennacherib's battles for him I do not know, but they were probably willing enough to take the chance of settling old scores against Judah. Were we not the country that had produced Saul and David, who had won so many battles against them in the past?

Nobody paid any attention to me, and I began to feel more confident. With such a gathering of different units and nationalities, it seemed I could always pass myself off as belonging to some other regiment if I were questioned, as this was quite likely to be the first time all the army had collected in one place. Now, from my vantage point slightly above the level of the camp, I could see that there was a steady progression of people towards the Royal Pavilion, so, taking a deep breath to steady my beating heart, I turned down the next alley and soon found myself one of a hurrying concourse of soldiers, workmen and camp-followers. As we drew near the clearing, and the crowd slowed and thickened, I found to my embarrassment that when my uniform was noticed, a way was made for me to press through; and glancing around I could see that no one round me wore the purple-and-gold patterned leather wristlets and long tunic that I had got on. Many wore rough hessian knee-length tunics, and were evidently not fighting men at all; and the soldiers wore the same sort of tunic as mine but with plain leather jerkins coming down to the hips, and unadorned leather shin guards and sandals.

Uncomfortably, I let myself be passed forward through the crowd, till I found myself standing just behind the single rank of spear-carrying guards who, as I had guessed, kept clear a rectangular space in front of the Royal Pavilion. Here, indeed, I found myself among what I took to be officers and young cadets like myself. One or two of them looked at me curiously, but fortunately they had other things to distract their attention. In front of the Pavilion, the great golden throne stood on a raised platform; behind it stood a semi-circular row of what I took to be high-ranking officers; and a little beyond stood a group of priests. A sacrifice must have just taken place, because the remains of a sheep's carcass lay on the ground, and a pool of hot blood lay steaming in the hollow of a stone altar. A sword-bearer stood with his reddened sword pointing to the altar, while the priests intoned various incantations, and some blew upon their horns. Suddenly I realized that at the far end of the rectangle, a detachment of soldiers was guarding some half-dozen prisoners—noteworthy because, although chained, they carried valuable-looking caskets, or statuettes in bronze and ivory, or ornaments of gold—and all were dressed in fine ceremonial robes.

There was a stir in the crowd, a moment's silence followed by a great shout and sounding of horns, and the King, Sennacherib the Terrible, strode out from his tent and mounted the throne. He sat impassively while an official proclaimed a long rigmarole about the greatness of Assur, god of the Assyrians, and of his servant Sennacherib, whose task of extending the dominion of Assur he had so nobly performed; and of the great acts he would continue to perform, and of the number of kings whom he had conquered and reduced to slavery, and of the fearful fate awaiting all other kings who dared to resist him, chief among whom at this time was King Hezekiah, shut up like a bird in a cage in Jerusalem.

From between the brawny arms of two guardsmen, I peered at the dark profile, half hidden beneath the great curled spade-shaped beard, above which the eyes glittered like coal. Two richly-dressed servants stood behind the throne, softly waving great fans of peacock feathers; the tips lightly brushed the King's helmet and as I watched absently I suddenly realized why the young Assyrian officers near me had been looking at me oddly. Alone of all those warriors, I was not wearing one of those pointed helmets. No doubt, this was a grand ceremonial occasion for which every soldier dressed in the full regalia to which his rank entitled him, and though presumably Adad was not the only warrior to lose his helmet in the stress of battle, everybody else around me, so far as I could see sliding my eyes nervously around, had made sure of a replacement.

This discovery so shook me that I lost track of what was

happening in the arena. Then I realized the speech-making had finished, and the captives were crawling forwards, on their knees, awkwardly clasping their offerings above their bowed heads. With a shock, I recognized one of these wretches as the Chief Ruler of Lachish, with whom my father had tried to carry out the Temple business, without much success. He had lounged about in his official residence, treating my father with the barest civility, and making no attempt to bestir himself on my father's behalf. Now as he crawled laboriously over the rough ground, sweat streamed from his white face. One of the other men looked vaguely familiar to me, but as for the rest, I could not tell whether they were Lachish men, or leading citizens brought here from some of the other cities captured round about. When they had made these offerings of their cities' wealth—purely a ceremonial gesture of submission, for the troops had looted all they wanted in the first two days—they were stripped of their fine robes and ordered to remain, kneeling, trembling and ridiculous, in nothing but their undershifts, before the throne.

Now came a sudden shift of attention. The King stood up and raised his arm. The priests began chanting again, but nobody paid much attention to them just then. Instead, all eyes turned to the battered walls of Lachish. I saw that a change had taken place in the last half-hour. When I had been coming down the valley, the great concourse of the army had swept like a sea right up to the very walls of the city, but at the time it seemed to me that the city itself was no longer an object of interest. I was wrong. Now everybody had withdrawn to the foot of the hill, but all eyes turned upon the double ring of fortification, battered but still largely intact.

Suddenly, from regular intervals all round the city, great columns of smoke arose from the perimeter of the inner walls, and shortly afterwards, a score of soldiers carrying burning brands came running out of the main gate and proceeded to encircle the outer walls. Now that I looked with closer attention, I could see that every thirty metres or so round the wall, the earth from the very foundations had been scraped away, and the walls themselves were supported on pit props round which dry firewood had been stacked. Evidently the wood had been soaked in oil or tar or some such material, because as each pile was touched by a burning brand, it roared up in sheets of flame, visible even in the bright noonday sun. One by one, the sections of wall above the inferno crumbled, the great rocks that had been shaped and heaved into place with such labour tumbling away down the slopes, leaving spaces through which we could see the inner wall collapsing in the same way.

I don't know how long we stood and watched, the soldiers bursting into loud cheers whenever a particularly large section of wall subsided, sending sparks shooting up to be lost in the dense cloud of smoke that hung over the entire city. At length Sennacherib raised his arm, and from all quarters of the great encampment men began to run towards the ruined defences; some took ropes and claw-like instruments, to heave at the broken edges of the walls; others were in teams carrying logs to use as battering-rams on the mud-brick walls of the common houses; the rest simply pulled burning logs from the fires and rushed into the city, to set alight the wattle roofs and every wooden structure they could find.

People, too small and distant to seem real, began to pour out of the smoking city and run helter-skelter down the slopes, and the sight of these panic-stricken refugees unleashed the last vestige of military discipline. All the soldiers not already ordered into the assault broke ranks and ran towards Lachish, their faces contorted with rage and glee, brandishing whatever weapon came to hand, or if they had none, shaking their bare fists and uttering hoarse screams like wounded stallions. Some set upon the fleeing wretches with stones and brands snatched from the fires; others rushed in over the scorching breaches in the walls to join in the orgy of destruction.

Sennacherib alone had remained still, seated upon his

throne, straight-backed and impassive save for a faint triumphant sneer upon his lips above the great black beard, the two slaves still waving the peacock fans above his head. Now he rose, and went to stand by the altar, above the pool of blood that flickered black and lurid gold in the light from the burning city. He held out his arms towards the funeral pyre of Lachish and cried out, 'Lo! Great Assur! Smile upon your sacrifice!' All those that remained, the officers and the priests and the bodyguards of tall spearmen, took up the chant: 'Lo! Great Assur! Smile upon your sacrifice! Lo! Great Assur! Smile upon your sacrifice!'

It suddenly occurred to me that I alone of the spectators remained with the King's entourage, and I turned to take cover among the rampaging soldiery.

I fell into the arms of a huge soldier who had been standing directly behind me. I looked up, startled, into the face, and recognized the fearsome red-lipped visage of the Assyrian who had threatened to throw me into the pit of the dead. Beside him stood one of the two sergeants who had spoken to Adad as we made our way up the valley with my father's body borne on Bathsheba. Some discussion about me must have taken place between them, because the sergeant simply nodded and the huge man nodded too, gazing piercingly into my face.

'Tell me, Jew-boy,' he said, 'where did you get that uniform?'

'From . . . from a dead Assyrian soldier.' Even in my terror, I felt a faint surprise at the question.

'A *dead* soldier?. . . Or a blind one?'

I glanced sideways at the sergeant.

'He was badly wounded. He died later.'

'Did he tell you his name?'

I hesitated, not out of any sense of loyalty to Adad but trying to work out, in a brain befuddled by fear, what answer would be most likely to help me.

'Adad,' I said. It did not matter either way; my case was hopeless.

The two men exchanged glances again, spoke to each other, and then the sergeant said, 'What did you do with the helmet?'

'He wasn't wearing one . . . or a sword.' I paused, and then added, desperately, 'He said he had run away. I suppose he had thrown his sword and helmet away.'

Why were these two men standing here questioning me, when they could so easily have killed me on the spot and joined their fellows in the sack of Lachish?

The big Assyrian's grip tightened round my throat. 'Assyrian soldiers do not run away,' he said. 'Now, listen carefully, if you wish to live. I am going to take you before the King, now, and tell him you are a Jew disguising yourself as one of his Youth Guards.' So that was what Adad was. 'You are to tell him that you took the uniform off a young wounded soldier as he lay dying on the battlefield, and that he told you his name was Adad before he died. Say that he was hit by an enemy boulder as he was leading an assault up one of the scaling ladders.'

I could not understand why saying any of this would help save my life, but I nodded feebly.

'Say it; say it now, to me.' Nervously I repeated the gist of what he had said. He nodded. 'That's good enough. Now, don't forget it; and if you say anything different, I will see that you are flayed alive.'

He handed me over to the sergeant, who gripped me firmly by the elbows and propelled me a few steps forward. The big Captain, for so I took him to be, advanced to a few paces before the throne, and saluted. The King signalled permission for him to speak, and after a brief conversation I saw him glance in my direction. Then the sergeant was summoned to bring me forward, and I found myself standing before Sennacherib the Terrible.

He looked me up and down, and laughed softly.

'So!' he said. 'A new recruit to my Youth Guards.'

I looked at my toes and said nothing.

With his sceptre he flicked the tasselled fringe of my

tunic, that hung too low, as I well knew, across my shins, and said, 'You should have found out first, that Sennacherib has no need to recruit babies to serve him. Nor,' he added with sudden violence, 'Jews!'

His gaze shifted from me to the spectacle of the burning city, as though he had already tired of the small diversion, and he went on, 'Now, tell me how you came to be wearing the uniform of Adad, son of the Rabshakeh.'

As I repeated the rigmarole the Assyrian Captain had taught me, I began to have some inkling of what all this was about, but nothing to give me any hope. Could this fearsome red-lipped giant who had so terrorised me at the edge of the mass grave, be the very Captain who, according to Adad, had cut him down so brutally in his flight beneath the walls of Lachish? If that were so, the man had every reason to want to hush up an episode which could have as uncomfortable consequences for himself as it would for the Rabshakeh's reputation. If it were the same man, he must have been pleased with the effect my words had.

'By his death the son of the Rabshakeh has brought honour to Assur,' the King commented, when I had finished. 'See that the uniform and insignia are given to the Rabshakeh on his return.'

Everything, including the bracelets, was stripped from me and I stood, a small and shivering wretch in nothing but a flimsy cotton loin cloth, with the burning city behind me and the greatest king on earth before me.

'What is the will of your Divine Majesty as regards the boy?' asked the Captain.

'Dispose of him how you like,' said the King indifferently, but then, as he gave me a second glance, he seemed to change his mind. 'Why do you suppose he came here?'

'As an enemy spy, no doubt,' said the Captain.

'A spy?' said Sennacherib, and he turned to speak directly to me. 'Are you a spy, boy? Are the Judaeans so short of men? And what do they need with spies, when a hundred thousand refugees flock to Jerusalem by the hour to report of our battle triumphs?'

'I am no spy,' I said. I remembered the terrible fate that befell the three Lachish scouts, and a cold faintness swept over me.

'And no peasant boy, either; a well-fed and well-spoken young spy.'

'I am no spy,' I repeated. 'I came here . . .' Why had I come here? Whatever the reason, I was repenting of it now. 'I came to see what was happening.'

Sennacherib stared at me a moment and then laughed aloud. The Captain joined in, but a trifle uneasily.

'So you note that, Captain? He is not a spy; positively not a spy; he just came to see what was happening.' He leant forward, and beckoned to me to come closer. I felt the sergeant's grip on my elbow relax, and I crept hesitantly forward. Sennacherib took hold of me and swung me round to face the burning city. 'I will show you what is happening,' he said. 'That is happening.'

It was a sombre sight, and more fearful than the picture of the burning city were the shrieks of the dying and the wailing of the bereaved. Nearly all the women and children had fled when I did, and most of the able-bodied men had been taken away in slave gangs. These I could see, now that most of the Assyrian host had dispersed, standing dolefully watching the death of their city and contemplating a fate worse even than mine—the long trek to a life of servitude in a foreign land. But some inhabitants had remained in the city, too old or ill, like the injured in the storehouse, to be worth the taking, or too useful to the invaders, like Joash and the baker, to be taken from their trades. What had become of Joash now? And his green fig tree, his reservoir of cool water, and his rows of precious pots? Those who came pelting out from the ruins now ran the risk of being cut down or shot by bowmen who hunted them like rats escaping from a granary. I wondered dully if Joash were among them, but fear for my own skin drove out all other emotions.

'Which of those houses is your home, boy?'

'None of them, Sir; I am not from Lachish.' No, I was not from Lachish; I was a citizen of the Holy City, one of God's Chosen, a member of the priestly tribe, and grandson of the great Isaiah. As I remembered these things, contempt for my own craven manner drove out fear, and new courage flowed through me. If I was to die, I would die worthy of my family and nation. 'I am from Jerusalem, of the tribe of the Levites, and grandson of the Chief Advisor of King Hezekiah.'

'Then you are the grandson of a foolish fellow,' remarked Sennacherib, but I could see that his interest had been caught. 'How do I know you are speaking the truth?' he asked suddenly, as though a thought had occurred to him which turned this minor amusement into something rather more important.

'You can ask the Chief Ruler of Lachish,' I said, pointing to the miserable figure of the prisoner, chained among his fellow-captives awaiting either death or transportation.

Sennacherib jerked his head in that direction, and the Captain went across and hauled the man before him. To be asked to indentify the son of the Temple Officer must have been the last thing the poor wretch expected, and I doubted whether he had paid enough attention to the quiet well-dressed boy who accompanied Shear-jashub on his official visit to recognize him in the half-naked lad who stood before him now.

He did, though. Perhaps it was just wishful thinking—I was obviously in deep trouble, and it must have offered a flickering ray of hope to him to be able, not only to assure the King that I was no product of Lachish, but even to identify me as the grandson of the famous prophet Isaiah. If he hoped to be rewarded for this piece of information, his luck was out; but mine was in.

'Go then, to your famous grandfather,' said Sennacherib. 'Go and tell him what you have heard and seen. Tell him that as Lachish is today, so will Jerusalem be tomorrow unless he gives better advice to King Hezekiah than he has been doing. I have heard of your prophet Isaiah, and of the great power he has over the King. Tell him that unless Jerusalem opens its gates to me, and yields up its treasures and its citizens unconditionally to my forces, that city will burn as Lachish is burning, and those inhabitants will perish or be led into captivity, as have the inhabitants of Lachish; and I will make the hill of Zion a place of desolation where only the jackal and vulture feed.'

I stood dazed, unable to comprehend my reprieve.

The Captain was less pleased. 'Sir,' he said, 'you have sent the Rabshakeh and his detachment to Jerusalem, and a hundred thousand refugees flock to the city with stories as persuasive as any this rogue can tell; if he really is the grandson of Isaiah, would not his head be a more powerful argument than any tales?' Up to now, the talk had all been in the Semitic tongue which was more or less common to both races, but the Captain had spoken his latest remarks in Aramaic, the language of the court and schools of learning. I suppose he had not wanted others to hear him differing from the King, and Sennacherib answered him in the same language. But I, brought up in the priestly school, had a pretty good knowledge of Aramaic, so understood much of a conversation that was not intended for my ears.

'You may be right,' said Sennacherib, and fresh fears shook me. To hope, and then have hope dashed thus. 'But,' he went on, 'they are strange people, the Hebrews, and may be moved in strange ways. The sickness in our camp is spreading, and our men have had enough of fighting. The vassal tribes are anxious to be home before the harvest, and there is unrest in the Babylonian provinces. If there is any way we can cut short this expedition without more battles, I would be glad of it, and if this boy here is a useful tool, then we may as well make use of him.' He turned to me, and changed back to the Semitic tongue.

'This time,' he said, 'Assur will spare you. The time may come, and soon, when you wish it had not been so. Be off, now, before his servant the King changes his mind.'

For a moment I stood still; then I turned and ran.

My instinct was to get away from anything Assyrian as quickly as possible, so instead of running back through the camp, I made straight for the olive groves on the hillside behind the Royal Pavilion. It was as well that I did, for before I had gone very far an arrow sang in the air beside me and stuck quivering in a tree trunk. Glancing back, I saw two bowmen on the slopes below me: one was running to cut me off; the other had his bow at full stretch, ready to loose off as soon as he had a clear view of me. The Captain, having extracted from me the story he had wanted Sennacherib to hear, had evidently sent a couple of his men to get rid of a dangerous witness as soon as I was out of Sennacherib's sight.

The men were some distance away, and I had the olive grove for cover. Some of the trees looked as old as the rocky soil to which they clung, their trunks huge and gnarled, and contorted boughs bent down to ground level, and while I was among them I felt reasonably secure. But if I kept on running upwards, I would soon be in open ground, and easy prey.

I paused behind one ancient tree, and looked about me. As I turned my head round, I had a momentary shock, for I thought I saw a shape like a man, or wild beast, standing absolutely still, an arm's length away. Then I realized it was just an old piece of cloth, grey and faded from exposure to the weather, left behind by some long-past olive harvester, and my heart beat again. I wondered about climbing into one of these great trees and hoping the bowmen would not think of looking up. But I was conscious of my white body, naked except for the loin cloth—it would be an impossible landmark to hide.

The old piece of cloth—ah, yes!

I leant out and ripped it from the bough where it hung,

but my action at once attracted the attention of one of the soldiers, who shouted to his fellow, and they began to run towards me. This tree, at least, would be no place to hide. I sped off, zigzagging between the trees and clutching the cloth to me, making for a particularly tangled-looking tree that promised good cover. The question was how to get there unobserved? Two more arrows sped by me, and I slipped under the protective canopy of the tangled tree I knew was too obvious a place to hide. However, beyond it lay a positive wilderness of interlacing neglected old trees, and my hopes rose.

As I crept from my first sanctuary I heard a dove cooing in the branches above me, and it gave me an idea. I edged on between the trees, being careful to make no noise or sudden movement, till I came to one that looked as though I could find a hiding-place in its branches. Before starting to climb, I picked up a good-sized stone and carried it with me as I scrambled up a long dipping branch into the first fork. From there it was easy to pull myself up into the next fork. Here a great branch had split many years before, and a gaping hollow had formed, fringed by a growth of young leafy shoots.

Before crouching down, I turned and flung my stone into the crown of the tree where I had first taken shelter. My ruse succeeded better even than I had hoped, for not just one or two but a whole flock of doves rose out of the branches with clattering wings, followed by the noise of the soldiers beating their way upwards through the tangled trees.

I slid silently down into the hollow, tucking the ancient piece of cloth around me. It was exactly the grey-green colour of olive bark and leaf, but I could have wished there were more of it, and that it was not so fragile, for I had to hold myself absolutely still and tightly huddled so as not to tear it or show any part of my body. I was soon in every kind of agony, both from my cramped position and the rough bark that cut into my unprotected skin, but I dared not move.

I found I could see a little through a slit in the old rag, but only upwards, into the leafy sky. It was, however, easy enough to tell where the bowmen were, because they made so much noise. After a short spell around the doves' tree, they scrambled about all over the wood, and, apparently, climbed to the upper limit of the grove to see if I had taken to the bare hillside.

They soon returned, and made a thorough search around the doves' tree—it sounded as though one of them climbed up into it. That frightened me, in case they should climb into my tree, too, but as I lay and stared up through the leaves with beating heart, a gaudy bee-eater suddenly hopped into my narrow field of vision, unconcernedly pecking among the twigs for insects. It was so close that I could have put out my hand and touched the golden and turquoise plumage; if the bird could come so close and not see me, I must be well hidden indeed, and when the soldiers passed right under my tree I felt scarcely a flutter of fear. The bee-eater flitted higher into the tree, and then flew on ahead of the men; shortly afterwards it returned to my branch and went on with its foraging, as though all danger had passed. I never see a bee-eater without recalling that friendly visitor, or feeling the sharp ridges of olive bark biting into my flesh, or smelling the mustiness of the old cloth covering my face.

I lay and listened to the footsteps of the soldiers, sometimes receding out of hearing, sometimes growing louder, but they never again came close. Darkness was falling, and as the daylight faded, so the red glow from the burning city brightened.

I stayed where I was, daring to shift my cramped body enough to ease the discomfort, but not to come down until it was fully night. Then I slid from my hiding place, tied the poor rag about my shoulders like a cloak, and made my way softly upwards to the edge of the grove, and so along the higher slopes to the place I had come to think of as home.

Chapter 6

One thing I discovered that night was that, even with no moon and a heavy blanket of cloud covering the stars, the blackness is never total. All the first part of my journey was illumined by the glow of burning Lachish, but even after the shoulder of the hill hid the ruins from me, leaving only a reddened column of smoke visible against the velvet dark, I could still see enough of the skyline to keep my sense of direction, though not well enough to find safe footing. As I stumbled along, I thought how carelessly I had dragged Adad up this valley, and shut my eyes to test the difference between total blindness and being sighted in the dark. After three steps I went sprawling, and gave up the experiment.

I wondered what Hannah and the others would be thinking. At least Adad would not see my humiliating return, stripped of his fine uniform and covering my nakedness with a torn rag; and I hoped Hannah would not have kept a lamp burning.

As I approached the place, picking my way carefully across the stream bed, I could see there was no light, but I was puzzled by an odd noise, like the sound of an incantation. On and on the voice went, in a dreary regular rhythm, apparently repeating the same words over and over again. It was an eerie experience and shivers shook my already cold body. I stood still and listened, trying to make out the words.

'"Oh Shamash, judge of Heaven and Earth, who establishes light for the people:
Oh Shamash, when you set, light is withdrawn from the people:
When you come forth, you bring warmth to all people:
The cattle and all living things that go out upon the wilderness, you give them life:
Oh Shamash, judge of Heaven and Earth who establishes light for the people . . ."'

The voice broke off and in the stillness I was certain the speaker was listening, as I was listening, each of us still, silent and alert.

'Adad?' I said softly.

A small relieved sigh reached me.

'Yes. Benjamin, is that you?' It was the first time he had spoken to me by name.

'Yes. What are you *doing*, Adad?'

'Tell me first, why are you so late? What happened? Are you all right?' His hand touched me as I came near, and felt along my bare chilled arm, and fingered the ragged piece of cloth where I had knotted it about my neck.

'They've taken your uniform,' I said. 'Gold bracelets and all. I am sorry.'

'How is it that you are still alive?'

First I had despised him, and later pitied him, but now I warmed to him as a friend. I had lost everything that linked him with his homeland, and he had let it pass without a word, his first concern my safety.

'I will tell you all about it,' I said. 'But where is Hannah? Is she asleep?'

'I think she must be. Is it night-time?'

I explained to him that it had been dark for at least two hours, and clambered over to the hut. Hannah sat outside, as she had sat last night, but this time weariness had overcome her. Blind as Adad in the deeper darkness by the wall, I had to feel her to find out where she was, and my touch aroused her. She started up with a cry.

'I'm back,' I said, 'and safe. I'll tell you about it in the morning. Lie down now; Adad and I can keep watch.' I felt weary, but very wide-awake. Perhaps I was too cold to be drowsy.

I urged Hannah to crawl into the shed and lie down with the children, and being only half-awake she submitted docilely. It meant she could share one blanket with them, and I could take the other one, which had been the old man's. Last night it had wrapped my father.

Adad had returned to his chanting.

"'You, the ghosts of my family, as many as lie in the underworld,
I have poured out water for you!
Stand before Shamash today, and judge my case!
The Bad Thing that is in my body, in my flesh, in the flesh of mine eyes, appoint over to the hand of Namtar, Messenger of the Underworld.
Sieze the Bad Thing, and send him down to the Land of No Return!
Let me your servant live and prosper!
Oh, Shamash, king of Heaven and Earth, who establishes light for the people!'"

He made some movements, crouching down, and feeling along the ground. Then he seemed to pick something up, and the incantation started again.

"'I give you as my substitute;
let the evil destined for my body be upon you;
let the evil before and behind me be upon you;
let this evil not return to its place upon Earth; let it not be near.'"

He broke off, and said in his natural voice, 'You must help me.'

I said, 'I'm not taking part in any sacrifice to *your* gods.' What would my grandfather say? More to the point, what would Jehovah say, who sees into the hearts of men?

'It's only to light the oil-lamp for me. I can manage the rest, I think.'

I lit the oil-lamp, telling Jehovah I was just lighting an oil-lamp, and that was all there was to it. Just a little light, no sacrifice. After all, I had lost Adad's gold bracelets.

I put the pottery lamp into Adad's hand, and he tilted it so that some of the oil spilt out on to a little pile of barley meal crumbs he had put in a heap on a flat stone. Then he held the light down, trying to set the crumbs alight.

'Are they burning?' he asked. 'Are they alight?'

'Sort of,' I answered. A drop of burning oil fell on to them, and they flared up for a moment and then went out, leaving a charred smell. Adad sniffed it and seemed satisfied. Then he began to feel around with one hand, still holding something carefully in the other.

'What do you want?' I asked.

'There's a jar of water somewhere here,' he said.

I could see it, just on the edge of the ring of light cast by the lamp, and I picked it up and gave it to him. He poured it over the scorched crumbs.

'"Bread I give you, and water I give you,"' he intoned.
'Shamash knows it is not the pure flour he loves.
Nor is the water from the rivers of his land,
from Tigris or Euphrates.
Shamash knows it is the best I can do!'

I wanted to laugh; his last words were obviously not part of the sacred text.

'Now,' he said, 'will you take me to the stream?'

It was hard enough for me to find my own way down into the stream bed, and leading Adad was made all the more difficult because he insisted on keeping his hands cupped over whatever it was he held in them. However, eventually we got there.

Adad was distressed to find so little water there, and large areas of dry shingle everywhere. When I guided his left hand down to a shallow pool, he scooped away as many small stones as he could with it—still clutching his treasure in his right hand—to deepen it. It reminded me of a dog burying a bone, and even more so when at last he stretched out his right hand and plunged both it and the thing it held into the depths of the pool, quickly shovelling the heap of pebbles back into the hollow, finally withdrawing his right hand with care, so as to leave the object safely anchored under the water and stones.

'Whatever was *that*?' I asked. It looked like a lump of mud, squeezed into the shape of some heavy-shouldered creature with wings or big ears, or perhaps tusks, from the brief glimpse I had had of it in the lamp-light; there was something horrible about it, which made me shudder.

'It is the blood-bull,' he said, shovelling in more pebbles. 'Can you find me a big stone, or two or three big ones?'

I put a couple of hefty boulders into his hands, and he laid them down in the water, carefully covering the mound of pebbles and pressing them down. Then he intoned some more about the Bad Thing, imprisoned for ever in the Land of No Return. Then he stood up, and felt for me.

'Thank you,' he said, in his normal voice, as I put my hand out for him. 'Now can you take me back?'

Bathsheba was lying down in the shed. I suggested we should sit out our watch tucked in between the warm donkey and the wall, covered in the blanket, which I now thankfully retrieved and wrapped around me. I made sure Adad had the wall and I had the donkey, because after all, he was, in a sense, my prisoner, *and* he was wearing my tunic.

'Now,' I said, when we were comfortably settled and I began to feel a welcome warmth spreading through me, 'What was all that about?'

He would not tell me at first, and asked instead about my adventures that evening.

I told him the whole course of events, and when I came to my arrest by a huge Captain, I asked Adad if he knew the man.

'Describe him to me,' he said, and I did. 'I think it could have been the man who slashed me across the face,' he said.

'That's what I wondered,' I said. 'But if he knew who you were, why did he do it?'

'I daresay he didn't know who I was,' he said. 'Not at the time. He was not my commanding officer. As one of Sennacherib's Youth Guards, I would normally have been with the King. But as my father had come ahead with the advance party to Lachish, I came with him, and there were a lot of different detachments under his command who did not know each other very well. But even if he *had* known me, he might not have recognized me; I'd have had my helmet on, and my hands to my face, and was covered in dirt and smoke and blood; besides, in battle like that, you don't have time to stop and think. His job was to keep the forces attacking, and if he saw anyone—*anyone*—running away, his instinct would be to drive them back, or kill them, for fear of a general rout.' He paused, and then added, 'I knew *him*, though. All the lads knew *him*. He'd been pointed out to me as the hardest man in the army; Captain Terror, they called him.'

I told him how the big Assyrian had seized me and threatened to throw me into the mass grave. 'That sounds like him,' he said, 'except that he didn't actually do it.'

He listened to the story of my encounter with Sennacherib, and my escape in the olive grove, and when I had finished he sighed and said, 'You must have been born under the protection of a lucky spirit.'

'I am under the protection of Jehovah,' I replied, like a good pupil of the priestly school, wondering in my heart why Jehovah had not chosen to protect my father.

'About my gold bracelets,' said Adad. 'It is the best thing that could have happened.'

'Why?'

'They will be given to my father, and he will recognize them for mine. He will believe what Captain Terror told you to say, about me dying a hero's death, and when he gets back home, they will say prayers for me, and praise my name, and be happy.'

'Happy? Your mother, too?'

'My mother is dead.'

'I am sorry.'

'I never knew her. She died giving birth to me. The demon Lamashtu crept in under the door like a mouse and stole away her spirit.' He paused a moment and then said, 'I think Narma-tani will be sad, but she will know it is for the best.'

'Who is she? Your grandmother?'

'No, one of my father's concubines. She was my father's favourite until he married the priestess Inishu, and then Inishu wanted to have her sold, because she was jealous of her. My father could not do that, because she had borne his children; but he had the slave-mark put upon her, to please Inishu. Before that, she would have helped me to persuade my father to let me study to be an architect, instead of training to be a soldier; she knew that was what I wanted.'

'But your father's new wife did not want you to?'

'No, of course not. Being a priestess, she thought it more fitting that I should be one of Sennacherib's Youth Guards, because that's what all the best families want for their sons; besides, as a soldier I'd be more likely to get killed, and then her sons would have more to inherit.' He paused a moment, and then said, 'I shall be sorry never to see Narma-tani again, but it is best this way. Her son Ibbi will miss me—we grew up together, and he would do anything for me. He is two years younger than me, you see; he must be nearly thirteen.'

'My age,' I said. That made Adad fifteen. It was young to embark on a life of darkness.

'What about the rest of your uniform?' I asked.

'That doesn't matter,' he said. 'Except that you now have nothing to wear.'

'Yes, I have.' I answered quickly. 'It's you who have nothing to wear.'

Unexpectedly, he laughed. It was only a little chuckle, but lying there in the dark beside him, unable to see his disfigured face, I glimpsed a different Adad, a cheery lad adored by his young half-brother and foster mother, who had perished outside the battlements of Lachish.

'Anyway, if I'm going to kill you, you won't need a tunic.' I tossed the remark out like a stone into a cave to see what wild creature lurked there before venturing in.

There was a sudden total stillness, and then Adad said evenly, 'Yes, of course. When are you going to do that?'

I felt compunction, but merely said, 'It was you who asked me.'

'I know.'

'Is that still what you want?' He said nothing. 'When I got back just now,' I went on, 'you were making some sort of sacrifice to your gods, weren't you?'

'It won't work,' he said. 'I hadn't got all the proper things, and I need a mashmashu to perform the rituals for me.'

'What's that then, a priest?'

'Sort of. A magic-man, a sorcerer priest. And the rituals have to be repeated every day for three days, otherwise you cannot be sure the demon is properly imprisoned in the blood-bull.'

I remembered the half-glimpsed winged lump that Adad had buried in the pool. It sounded very like the kind of hocus-pocus my grandfather was always condemning among our peasant people, though it was not the simple countrymen he got angry with so much as the tricksters who played upon their superstitions to make themselves fat livings. I was surprised that anyone of Adad's sophisticated background should dabble in such stuff. Then I remembered my father's tale of King Ahaz, burning his two-year-old son as a sacrifice, and decided I would not mock.

'Why do you call it a blood-bull?'

'It has to be made of dust and blood; the blood should be that of a bull, and the dust should come from a ruined town, a ruined temple, a grave, a neglected garden, a neglected canal and a disused road.'

'That's a bit complicated,' I said. 'Where did you get the dust from?'

'Joel fetched it for me. He got some from the road, and some from the stream bed, and some from the cucumber patch—he said that was neglected enough—and some . . .' He broke off.

'Whose grave?' I said.

'It wasn't your father's. Joel said an old man is buried here, too.'

'I don't suppose he'll mind,' I said, relieved. 'What about the blood?'

'Joel said there was some mixed up with the dust from the building.'

That would be the old man's, too. I wondered if Joel had told him it was human blood, but said nothing.

Adad went on, 'Then you have to mix it all up and make it into the shape of the demon who is troubling you.'

'Do you know what he looks like?'

'No. There are so many; thousands. But I gave it four wings, and cloven feet, like the demon Pazazu, because he's a particularly evil demon, and I know what *he* looks like. At least I tried to, but how do I know? I never saw it.'

'Joel could have told you.'

'When Hannah discovered what Joel was doing, she got very angry, and wouldn't let him come near me. That's why I had to wait till they were all asleep before I could say the spells; and *that* was all wrong too. How can Shamash the sun god hear me when he has gone down behind the rim of the world?'

'Our Jehovah can hear us by day or night, for he has made them both and is Lord of All Things,' I said.

'Then nobody in Lachish can have been praying,' said Adad pointedly, and I had no answer at the time, though later I remembered what Isaiah kept telling us about the Assyrians being God's chosen weapon of chastisement.

However, it was other things that were troubling Adad.

'I should do it by daylight, three times, each time the sun comes up; and wrap the idol in a lion skin, and hang a precious stone round its neck, and cover it with a pot upside-down over a tripod, and a lot more things; otherwise how can I be sure the demon will not escape from under the boulder in the river? *And*,' he added, as though it were the last straw, 'I'm sure I didn't burn the right kind of flour.'

'Do you think all this is going to get you back your sight?' I asked.

'If I'd done it *properly* . . . I don't know. But what else can I do?' He sighed despondently. 'There are so many demons.'

'But you know perfectly well no demon blinded you. It was the burning brands, and the big Captain with his sword. They are the only demons you have to look for.'

'*They* are not going to give me back my sight,' he said.

'Nor is burying imaginary demons in bits of mud,' I said.

For the second time that night he went very still, and when, after a long silence, he spoke again, it was in that same cold level tone of voice that he had used when I tossed off the suggestion that I should kill him.

'Because I am blind, and cast out by my own people, and alone in a foreign land, you think you can kick me around like a toothless dog,' he said.

I stirred uncomfortably, but the edge of menace in his voice irritated me. I was quite prepared to be kind to him so long as he knew his place.

'That's right,' I said.

Suddenly he was upon me. Strong hands gripped my throat and with his knees pressing against my ribs he held my hands pinioned under the blanket. Desperately I struggled to force my arms free, but in vain; pain tore at my lungs as I fought for breath. I was conscious of Adad's face with its terrible scars barely an inch from mine, but when he spoke, his voice, although barely a whisper, seemed to come booming from an immense distance, till the singing in my ears and my pounding heart drove out all other sounds.

'A man does not need a sword to kill,' he breathed, 'nor the sight of his eyes, not if he is angry enough. You think I have no right to anger, no right . . . no right . . .'

I do not know whether he stopped speaking or I lost consciousness. All I remember is a feeling of limpness taking hold of every part of my body and an unbearable throbbing in my head, behind my eyes. Blackness engulfed me, and my last conscious thought was, 'His demon has given me his blindness.'

I do not think I was unconscious for long—maybe not more than a few seconds. I became aware of a regular tearing noise, very loud and very close; then it seemed to fall into step with stabs of pain and a strange sensation that my whole body was swelling up to huge proportions, then shrinking to nothing, in time with the pain and the tearing noise. As my brain cleared, I knew it was my breathing.

I never thought to call out for help. I rolled over and buried my face in Bathsheba's musty back, and cried. I realized dimly that the weight that had pinned me down so unmercifully was gone, and gingerly I lifted my hands to my aching throat. My whirling thoughts began to settle.

Where was Adad? Did he think he had killed me? Was he hovering nearby, waiting to finish me off if I showed the slightest sign of life? No, my rending breaths and my sobs would assure him I was not dead, unless he had run away. Where, though, could he run to?

'Adad?' I whispered, tremulously.

'I am here.' The voice came from beside me. He had scarcely moved.

I turned and felt for him in the dark, as a blind man would do. He let me touch him unresponsively. I took my hand away and lay there, quiet, knowing the danger was past, and wondering.

'What . . . what was that for?' I asked at last.

'You made me angry,' he said.

'You nearly killed me!' I wished my voice were not shrill-edged with shock.

'I am sorry. I did not mean to.' His voice, too, was high and strained, but then I heard him turn his head towards me, and repeat, naturally, 'I did *not* mean to. You must believe me.'

'I don't see why I should.'

'Because if I *had* meant to kill you, I could have done it, easy.'

'All right. But I don't see what right you've got to be angry.'

'No,' he said, harshly. 'Blind men have no rights. They stand at street corners, staring sightlessly up into the sky, holding out a bowl for charity. And when someone drops in some bread, or a coin, they whine their gratitude, and if someone steals their bread, the only right they have is to fall down and die in the gutter.'

'In our country,' I said thoughtlessly, 'a man's family do not let him die because misfortune has come upon him.'

'I think,' he said, steeling himself, 'it would be best if you kill me. Only don't joke about it, as though it is a thing of no importance. I don't suppose it matters much to you, but it is the only life I've got. Sometimes I forget I have nothing left, just for a few minutes, and then you remind me; or sometimes I think there is a little hope, that maybe I have captured the demon and will see again, and then you laugh at me and say it is not so.'

'Perhaps you will get your sight back,' I said, 'but not by burying demons. We have healers and holy men in our country. There are clever doctors in Jerusalem who might be able to help you.'

'Help me? An Assyrian?'

'My father helped you.'

'Yes,' he said. 'If he had not been your father, I think I might have killed you just now.'

'If it were not for my father, I would have left you to die.'

'Listen,' he said. 'You talk of Jerusalem as though you

expect to go back and find it the same as when you left it.'

'Yes,' I said. 'I had forgotten.' It was true. My own experiences in the past few days had been so intense and overwhelming that I had scarcely given a thought to the national tragedy that was being played out all around us.

'If your King does not yield to Sennacherib, he will burn it to the ground like Lachish, and carry away all your people into captivity.'

'And what if he does yield?'

'I don't know. He'll probably still send away all your young men to be slaves in Assyria, but maybe he'll leave the city standing, so long as your King pays him enough, and does him homage.'

'I hate him,' I said. 'Why does he have to come trampling and destroying our land? Why can't he stay in his own country?'

'It is the honour of Assur,' Adad replied. 'Or the honour of Sennacherib. Me, I wanted to raise buildings up in honour of the gods, not burn them down. Like you said in your father's funeral prayers—swords into spades, and not training young men to fight any more.'

'It will come,' I said. 'Maybe.'

'Too late for me,' said Adad.

A long silence fell between us, but it was not a silence between enemies. I was trying to think what I could say to give him hope, but could find nothing. I kept thinking of our great hero Samson, the strong man taken prisoner by the Philistines after he had let a woman betray him. They had put out his eyes and left him to grind corn as a slave, blind among enemies. His answer had been to use his great strength to pull down the pillars of their temple so that the building fell upon them all, killing hundreds of people, and himself with it. Adad did not want to pull buildings down, but to raise them up.

'I'm not going to kill you,' I said suddenly. 'Nor talk about it any more. That's a promise. So the next thing is to try and find some way of getting your sight back. Things like you being an Assyrian and me being a Judaean, or what happens to Jerusalem, we can't do anything about. But I've got to get back to my family, to let them know I'm alive, and see if they need help, and tell them about my father; so you'd better come with me, and we'll just have to see what happens when we get there.'

'Yes,' said Adad. 'I have to say thank you.'

'You don't have to,' I said, a little stiffly.

'Yes, I do. But I don't like doing it, so I'm not going to pretend about it.'

At the time, I felt rebuffed. I had made what seemed to me a fair and generous undertaking. Adad was an enemy, a prisoner and a cripple, totally in my power; what is more, he had just snatched a moment when I had let myself be vulnerable, to attack and very nearly kill me. I lay there in silence, astonished at my own magnanimity and Adad's graceless response, feeling noble because I would not break my promise there and then, when the words were scarcely out of my mouth.

Adad must have guessed at my thoughts, for after we had lain unspeaking and apart for fully half an hour, he suddenly broke the silence.

'I could have lied to you just now,' he said. 'Easily. I could have crawled before you, saying how noble and generous you are and how I would be your servant for the rest of my life, and you could put your foot on my neck; that's how all the politicians talk. But it seemed to me that you had spoken the truth from your heart, and you deserved better than lies from me. I am sorry if what I said hurt you, but friendship and gratitude are two different things. You have to choose one or the other.'

If I had been among my own people, with my nation's hate for all things Assyrian pressing in on me on every side, if it had been daylight, and I could have seen Adad for the blinded creature that he appeared to be, I believe even then I would have made the stupid, arrogant response. But it was dark, and we were alone with the stars and the patient donkey and the near presence of my father's spirit.

'I'll choose friendship,' I said.

PART TWO

Chapter 7

Hebron, when we got there, was a pile of rubble from the cracks of whose ruined buildings peered hungry, frightened faces—refugees too young, too old or too sick to drag their few possessions the twenty miles north to the doubtful safety of Jerusalem.

'Have the Assyrians taken Jerusalem?' we asked.

Nobody knew, but a few shook their heads doubtfully. No news had come through that Jerusalem had fallen; a steady stream of fleeing families had passed that way; none had returned.

Joash had told Hannah to wait for him in Hebron, but Joash in all probability was dead, or enslaved, and Hebron looked like a field of sesame after a cloud of locusts had passed that way. Waves of refugees had flooded into the village, only to flee into the hills at the approach of the Assyrians and return, fearfully, after the destroying forces had moved on, to glean every poor grain of corn and unripe fig they could find remaining.

Food for ourselves became a matter of life and death. I had a little money, so had Hannah; but there was nothing for our money to buy, and the food Joash had sent was all gone. To go south into the red desert of the Negev, now, as late spring gave way to the parching drought of summer, would be madness; and the barren hills that lay between us and the great trough of the Dead Sea to the coast were just as inhospitable. There was nothing for it but to follow in the steps of the thousands ahead of us, and make for Jerusalem. At least if we got there safely, and the city was neither under siege nor burnt to the ground, I would be reunited with my family and they would see that my companions did not starve. Nevertheless, we had all, Adad included, experienced too many terrors on the battleground of Lachish to feel easy at the prospect of hurrying towards their likely repetition.

Our first sight of Jerusalem, as we looked down from the hillside after passing the battered settlement at Bethlehem, relieved our worst fears. The city appeared to be still standing, and there was no sign of the Assyrian army encamped between us and the slopes of Mount Zion on which it stood. I could clearly see the walls of the Temple shining golden in the setting sun, beyond the tall towers of the King's Palace on nearby Mount Moriah. Tucked away behind the great artificial mound Solomon had thrown up to give grandeur to his palace lay the priest's dwellings. Although I could not see them, the sight of my familiar city brought so clear a picture of them to my mind that I could visualize the life going on there as vividly as if I stood in our own green and shaded courtyard.

As I stood and stared out across the Hinnom valley, I felt enclosed, as in a bubble of unreality. I recalled the eager boy, setting forth, washed and dressed in a smart new tunic, listening to his mother's instructions with half an ear while the two servants adjusted the loads on the donkeys and his father stood by, patient and smiling.

'You mind you do everything your father tells you; there are not many fathers as easy-going as your father and I'm not having folk out in the country getting false ideas about us city-dwellers. You needn't smile, Shear-jashub; if those country priests see what freedom you allow your son and servants, they'll take advantage of you in every way. You just let them know who's in charge; and make sure Benjamin says his prayers and attends all the sacrifices. Oh, I know what your father has to say about that; but out there, and you a representative of the Temple, it won't do, and you know it. And you be careful about mixing with the local boys, Benjamin; and don't go tearing that good tunic. And see he goes to bed in good time, Shear-jashub. . . .' I remembered seeing the servants glance at each other, with amused smiles. If Shear-jashub needed practice in displaying authority, he was not likely to get it in his own courtyard.

What had happened to that boy? Under the dirt, I felt the lines of my face drawn from hunger and cracked from exposure; with the servants and the animals had gone any pretensions to status; and my smiling father lay under a heap of stones in a neglected cucumber field. I still wore my good new tunic, taken back from Adad whom we had clothed, easily enough, from bundles of possessions discarded by refugees, too tired to carry them further or fleeing from bandits. But my tunic, torn, bloodied, soiled and sweaty, worn by an enemy and ritually unclean from contact with the dead, was as different from the fine linen garment I had set forth in as I was from the boy that had worn it.

The tunic would have to be burnt. Strange that I had not given a thought to any of the religious consequences of my actions until now, when the sight of my own city brought back all the old accepted traditions. Anyone who touched a dead body had to begin a series of rituals three days afterwards, and was not classed as 'clean' until seven days had passed. It was already five days since I had buried my father, nearly seven since I had dragged the body of the old man away from the doorway of the hut. There were all kinds of regulations, too, for the cleansing of warriors who had been in battle, but whether they applied to me I was not sure. No doubt my mother's uncles would know, for she came of the true priestly family, descendants of Aaron. My father was merely accepted as a Levite by virtue of the high standing granted him as a son of the great prophet Isaiah. I had a feeling they would all have a heyday with me, carrying out every last detail of religious ritual, unless my powerful grandfather saw fit to interfere.

We had made slow progress from Lachish. At first, Hannah had ridden the donkey, with Adad holding the pannier for guidance. Joel had run along pretty well, but I had had to carry Rebecca for long stretches, because Bathsheba was too burdened with the water pots and the provisions sent by Joash to be able to take the child as well. It was not a very satisfactory arrangement, chiefly because Bathsheba, while picking her own way delicately enough between the boulders, led poor Adad at her side into one painful booby-trap after another. Joel was told to lead him instead, and performed the task quite well for a time, but he was much too lively and impatient to keep at it for long. It was Rebecca who came to Adad's rescue.

'Look where you're *going*, Joel,' she cried crossly from my shoulders. 'Please, can I lead Adad? Can I? Can I?' From then on she guided him tenderly and with grave attention, sometimes from her perch on my back, but usually on foot. She enjoyed her role so much that she was able to walk much longer distances than before without getting tired; and although we still moved along very slowly, at least it was not to the sound of Adad's stifled groans and curses. He had felt the ignominy of his position, as well as physical pain; he was so obviously a burden to the rest of us; but he did not mind being led by Rebecca. She made him feel he was conferring a privilege on her, and I was reminded of how confidently she had handled Joel when he had that fit on the hillside.

Joel was a strange boy, full of wiry energy, excitable and unpredictable; sometimes he would fall into deep glooms without warning, and as suddenly emerge from them. His mother said she had taken him many times to the priest of the illegal High Place at Lachish, and performed sacrifices and cleansing ceremonies to rid him of whatever devils were troubling him, but without much result. I couldn't see there was anything very wrong with him—it was just the way he was; but Hannah was as superstitious in her way as Adad was in his. Perhaps that was why she disapproved so strongly of his religious rituals; I was content to laugh at them inwardly, but she, I think, was genuinely afraid that he might invoke hostile powers and bring the wrath of our own Jehovah upon our heads. And yet she saw nothing wrong in making her own prayers and little offerings to all kinds of spirits and was concerned about my impiety because I would not meddle with such things.

All the same, underneath this fussing about sacred rites, there was a deep tranquillity about Hannah. The rituals were just things she had been taught to perform, in the same way as she had been taught how to grind corn or spin wool; they were part of her daily routine, not part of herself. If the wool was there, she would spin it; if the corn was there, she would grind it; but if they were not there, then she accepted hunger and cold as part of life that must be endured. In the same way, she dutifully propitiated a host of demons and spirits as occasion arose, but when disaster befell her she accepted it without any sense of clawing guilt. Her emotions were simple and direct; terror when the drunken soldiers abducted her, grief for her dead baby, anxiety about the fate of Joash, and protective love for her remaining family, among whom, without question, she included a sprig of the arrogant priesthood from Jerusalem—for so Lachish dwellers no doubt saw me—and a blinded enemy soldier. I took a good deal of quiet credit to myself for not deserting these helpless refugees, but I never wondered at the way this destitute woman took Adad and me under her wing. The outlook for her must have been black indeed: a widow, for all she knew, far from her own tribe, separated from her husband's people by the fortunes of war, moving in the wake of hordes of refugees who had already stripped the land of everything that could support life, towards a city surely soon to be destroyed: and with two small children dependent on her for their lives.

Later, back in the clever, snarling rivalries of the Temple precincts, it was suggested to me that Hannah had cared for me out of cunning, hoping to earn herself merit in the eyes of an influential family; but I think my sharp-tongued relations were wrong. If such a thought had crossed her mind, her first impulse would have been to dump Adad, but she never showed the slightest sign of wishing to be rid of him, or, indeed, of treating him like an outsider; she mothered him as she mothered me, accepting and giving without reserve.

It was almost dark as we dropped into the valley of the Kidron brook where it joins the Hinnom, and climbed the short steep slope up to the Dung Gate. We were a hungry weary group. Hannah was walking now, though limping painfully. The two children were slumped on Bathsheba's back, limp from exhaustion and lack of food. Adad's face was set in grim lines of pain; he had hardly spoken at all these last two days, and it was clear from the tightly-stretched discoloured skin around the sword wound across his left eye that infection had set in. The other, burnt, side of his face, though it looked badly disfigured, seemed to trouble him less. It was I who guided him into Jerusalem, while Hannah supported the sleepy children and led the donkey.

Even I, who had known the city since infancy, was in danger of losing my way, because it appeared totally strange. Every handsbreadth of space was packed with people. They slept huddled on the roadway, they crouched under makeshift tents slanted against the walls, they overflowed into every courtyard. Some had lit small fires, more to keep off the evening chill than to prepare food upon, because their silence and lack-lustre movements, their pale faces and hollow eyes, spoke of days without food.

We forced our way over and between the carpet of bodies, and I expected the crowds to thin out a little as we left the gateway behind us, and the steps around Hezekiah's new water supply at the Pool of Siloam, but they did not. Every alley and street was full of people; they had set up their little encampments right against the buttresses of the Palace Mount, and only the soldiers on guard can have prevented them clambering up and spilling over into the royal grounds. It was the same when we eventually reached the Temple precincts, and when at last I had battled through the throng to reach our own courtyard, I was not surprised to find the gate bolted and barred, as every priest's house had been that we passed.

I beat upon the gate, and shouted; dulled eyes turned to stare at me and my tattered companions, thinking, no doubt, that we looked more fit to share the dusty street with the other refugees than to expect entrance to the priest's courtyard.

I scarcely expected my voice to carry above the mingled noises of the people and animals thronging the roadway, but I was wrong. Almost immediately our old servant, Abraham, appeared over the wall, looking down at me. All he said to me was, 'I'll open the gate immediately,' but as he climbed down out of sight I could hear him shouting, 'The master's son is here; he's come back.' They had kept a look-out for me and my father, day and night; I had not thought of that.

Abraham opened the gate cautiously, and while he drew me in, he kept peering into the darkness beyond me, oil-lamp in hand, as though expecting a surge of gate-crashers; but the refugees in the street just watched the proceedings dully, as though they had grown accustomed to rebuffs.

'You must let these people in,' I said. 'They are my friends.'

'If they are friends of my master's son, they are welcome,' replied Abraham, but he looked doubtfully at the little party, and closed the door quickly on Bathsheba's heels as though still afraid that a mob might rush the gate.

'We are so many here already,' he began apologetically, for he knew I would be remembering that in all my life I had never known our doors locked against strangers or beggars. Indeed, the courtyard was full of donkeys and heaps of baggage, and a group of unfamiliar servants appeared to have taken over one end of the courtyard as their sleeping quarters. However, I had no time to ask what they were doing there, as my mother came running out of the house and crushed me to her in her strong arms. Then she held me away from her, and looked searchingly into my face.

'Your father?'

I had practised a hundred ways of facing that question, and always as the strong one, breaking news to which I had become accustomed to a shocked weak widow. Now, held in my mother's arms like a child, I could not speak; tears welled up in my eyes and I crumpled against her like a baby.

She stroked my head, and began the controlled ritual wailing for the dead; my aunts and sisters who had clustered round joined in, and the old men began to groan and tear their clothes. The familiar Jewish celebration of grief swept me up in a great releasing of emotion, and I looked up, unashamed of the sobs tearing at my chest. Hannah was wailing aloud in natural communion with those around her, able at last to pour out her love for her dead baby. Joel and Rebecca stared around, befuddled with sleep and grizzling with exhaustion. Only Adad stood still and pale, his face set.

After a while, it seemed proper to my mother to draw a curtain over the public mourning. 'Come in,' she said, and the wailing died away. 'You must eat and rest, and then tell us everything.' She heaved a tremulous sigh, and said resolutely, 'God is good, who has sent me back my first-born son from the dead.' As she hugged me again, her eyes strayed over my companions.

'These people have been my friends,' I said. It was not much of an explanation, but it had served to get them into the courtyard, and now they would be accepted. They were 'the strangers within our gates', and as such assured of hospitality.

'You are welcome,' said my mother, and her brothers came forward to repeat the words. 'You may share what we have, food and drink, bed and board; but you must understand that at this time, it is not much.'

'I understand, and I thank you,' said Hannah, with grave simplicity.

I could not help but see how all the eyes kept turning, enquiringly, on the silent blind youth, sensing something strange and alien about him. They saw his blank disfigured face, but that was not it; they observed his complete silence, but that was not it, either. Something, something hung in the air like an unseen curtain, a frosty suspicion withering compassion to its roots.

'This is Adad,' I said, and the foreign name stabbed the air like an icicle. 'He was blinded in the battle of Lachish, and he was with my father when he died.'

'You are welcome,' said my mother briefly, but the silence that followed was too long. I have never seen anyone look so lonely, ever.

It was Rebecca who saved him. One of the uncles had lifted her off the donkey and was cuddling her in his arms. Now fully awake, she wriggled to escape. 'Put me down,' she said. 'I have to lead Adad.' Taking him by his unresponsive hand, she turned trustingly to my mother. 'Where do we go?' she asked.

I was too tired that night to take in very much, and too tired to eat more than a few mouthfuls, although I had been thinking of that meal all day; but I was dimly aware that the sour milk and meal cakes formed an unusually frugal meal for my mother to set before guests. I was also aware of the vast concourse of relations that spilled over into every room. It was all their servants whom I had seen encamped in the courtyard along with their pack-animals and even a few goats. Sheer self-defence had compelled my mother to lock out the hordes of refugees on the streets, but no Judaean family would refuse entry to relatives, and they had come pouring in from every village as the Assyrian menace drew near.

In the morning, I learnt more. Just as our home lay in a state of siege, so did Jerusalem, although no great army encircled it. The Rabshakeh had come to the gates, demanding surrender. Hezekiah had taken all the vessels of gold and silver from the Temple, including the seven-branched candlesticks and even the great winged cherubim from the Holy of Holies; he had stripped his own palace of the carved ivories and precious ornaments worked by Phoenician craftsmen employed by King Solomon, and had given them to the Rabshakeh to take back to Sennacherib as tribute. Now all Jerusalem waited to hear whether Sennacherib the Terrible would be satisfied with treasure, or whether he would send his great army up from Lachish to destroy the capital, as he had destroyed forty-six other walled cities of Judah. Like a great cat he lay, watching his prey, the injured mouse, hobbling away; with one lazy paw he could scoop it back to be crunched in his jaw or, if he felt sated enough, he might sleep, and let the damaged creature slink off into its hole.

In the meantime, while his soldiers roamed the countryside ransacking and burning crops, thousands of dispossessed peasants converged upon the one city not yet razed to the ground; the population of Jerusalem had more than trebled in the three weeks since I had left, and still the refugees came pouring in. King Hezekiah had enlarged the walls on the southern side of the city some years before, so that they encircled both the old city on Mount Zion and the Palace, the Temple and the priests' dwelling on Mount Moriah, and crept down the slopes as far as the Hinnom ravine; now he was using all available labour to throw up an outer wall well to the north to protect his people, but everyone knew it was a useless gesture. If Sennacherib chose to lay seige, he would use a weapon no walls could withstand: famine.

Our household was probably as well provisioned as any in the city, and could afford the inflated prices merchants were asking for their diminishing stocks of grain and oil; but soon there would be no food for anyone to buy.

The countryside had been devastated, as Hannah and I knew from experience; and even our household could not survive long on its reserves with so many mouths to feed.

Nevertheless, my mother accepted Hannah and the

children without question. The fact that Hannah had befriended me would have been enough to ensure their welcome, but the plight of the children appealed to my mother's generous heart, and Hannah did her best to be useful in a house where already too many servants were falling over each other.

Adad was a different matter. He could not remain silent for ever, and as soon as he opened his mouth he would betray his Assyrian origins. I summoned up courage next morning to explain how he came to be with me, though I said nothing about the Rabshakeh being his father, or about how he nearly strangled me. I made as much as I could of how he had held my father in his arms during his last hours, and how it was only with his help that I had been able to carry my father's body away for proper burial, and how he came by his second injury. I am not sure that the latter incident did much for his reputation; a cowardly Assyrian was no better, in my relations' estimation, than a cruel one. The absurdity of sharing one's last crust with a member of the hostile force intent on destroying and starving one did not escape them; blindness, moreover, meant a life of beggary unless you had a family to support you. At best, Adad was an embarrassment, and at worst, his very existence was an insult.

So thought my uncles, aunts and grandparents; and my elder sisters simply could not bear to look at him. But though it went against the grain, my mother stood by him, for my sake and the sake of those dark hours outside the walls of Lachish. She could not bring herself to like him, but out of a kind of fear she had of displeasing my father's spirit—a fear she had never displayed when he was alive—she steeled herself to do her best for him.

That included summoning the best doctor Jerusalem could provide to treat his injuries. He pronounced the eye slashed by the big Captain so badly infected as to be poisoning the whole face; so he removed it, and cauterized the wound, and laid poultices of dried figs upon the place. Adad endured the excruciating pain stoically, and in due course the wound healed cleanly and gave no further trouble; but all hope of regaining sight in that eye, whether by miracle healing or spells to get rid of demons, was gone for ever.

When his other eye, still sightless, began to give him headaches in the bright sunshine, and the doctor proposed removing it also, Adad refused, preferring hope to freedom from pain. Hannah had spoken to him of a holy man, living in the city of Samaria in the Northern Kingdom, who had performed great miracles. If we escaped from our present predicament, that was where he should go, she told him, and he clung to that hope, along with one other. This was that if he laid low till the Assyrian host had departed, he might be able to find a mashmashu, an Assyrian sorcerer-priest, among the garrisons dotted about the Northern Kingdom and, for all we knew, Judah itself, who could carry out all the proper incantations and sacrifices to rid him of the demons of blindness. So the doctor advised stitching the eyelids together, to keep out the bright glare and the dust and to protect it from unseen injuries, and to this Adad agreed.

Meanwhile, I was made to undergo all the rituals necessary for my cleansing, including the sacrificing of one of the goats. On that day at least we ate meat, gathered round the great copper altar in front of the Temple, but with all the male members of the household in attendance, and the women waiting below for their share afterwards, one goat made for meagre portions. Since my priest uncles officiated, they came in for a double share—their dues as priests and their rights as members of the household. The fat, of course, was burned along with the entrails on top of the altar, after the blood had been thrown against the side walls; but the poor goat was so skinny that not much flame ascended to the nostrils of the Almighty. The atmosphere of austerity was enhanced by the state of the Temple. Although the great columns, Jachin and Boaz, still stood towering above the Temple rooftop, they had been stripped of the golden pomegranates and lilies which I had so often wondered at, clustering thickly all over them; and much of the copper had been torn away from the Molten Sea, the huge water cistern supported by twelve copper bulls. The ivory and cedarwood carvings had gone from the porch, and my priest uncles told us that the ornaments had been taken from the Holy Place, and even from the Holy of Holies beyond it. Such sacrilege shocked them to the core, but it did not spoil their appetites for their double portions. Later, rosy from the wine and full of good meat, they swam behind their lordly paunches from the Temple to my father's house, and the wan refugees watched them pass with awe, but crept forward with begging hands outspread to the rest of us who followed.

Adad, not being one of Jehovah's people, and Hannah as a woman, had not shared in the cleansing ritual, but had been given their portions of meat along with the other women, children and servants, and had gone home ahead of us. When I got back, I found Joel and Rebecca telling Adad about every detail of the Temple that they could remember. He seemed extraordinarily interested, and asked me to fill in all sorts of measurements, the length and height of the building, the number of side-chambers, and the dimensions of the forecourt.

'Joel tells me it is only thirty or so paces for a grown man, from end to end,' he said. 'That cannot be true. Perhaps that is just the ante-chamber?' He began to tell me about the great new capital Sennacherib was building at Nineveh, ringed by a massive wall eight miles long, with fifteen gateways. Not every building had been completed; that would be a task for the slave labour Sennacherib would be driving home before him. As he described them, he sketched out their shapes with his hands, and became more animated than I had yet seen him. 'The temples in Khorsabad and Nimrud would make your Temple look like a porch,' he said. 'And in every village we have holy shrines bigger than that. But then,' he added, 'we have so many gods, and every god expects his temple to be bigger and more glorious than the other.'

I said his gods sounded like spoilt children, and to my surprise, he agreed. 'But think what it is to be an architect in Assyria!' he exclaimed.

'Yes,' I said. 'All those foreign slaves to work to death heaving stones about, and fine ivories and golden ornaments stolen from other countries to decorate your temples and palaces.'

He went quiet and stiff then, and remembering my lesson that night outside the cucumber shed, I left him alone.

From sunset that night I was considered 'clean', and the very next morning my uncles Shebna and Joah were to take me to the Palace for an audience with the King, to deliver my message from Sennacherib. I could not see much point in it. As the big Captain had so truly said, when refugees were flocking, terror-stricken, into Jerusalem from every walled city razed to the ground by the Assyrians, the testimony of one boy was of no value; but my uncles said it was my duty to report all I had seen. I think the truth was they were anxious to buttress their influence at court. There was a younger priest, Eliakim, who was making a name for himself as one of the King's counsellors, and who had the advantage of being the son of the Master of the King's household; and my uncles were anxious not to be edged out of the King's favour. Everybody knew that the only person whose judgement Hezekiah really trusted in moments of crisis was my grandfather Isaiah. My uncles, as my mother's brothers, could claim no direct relationship with the great prophet, but at least, now that Shear-jashub was dead, they could present themselves as guardians of his grandson.

Nobody had seen Isaiah. Some said he was closeted with the King in his Palace; some thought he was staying in our house; others that he had fled into the desert, knowing that Sennacherib would pay a handsome reward for his head. I felt pretty sure that he would be striding the barren hills between Jerusalem and Jericho, wrestling with Jehovah for a religious answer to a political crisis. Other people's grandfathers played a prominent part in ruling over their families, but not my grandfather. He thought in terms, not of boyhood and adolescence, of family finances and marriage settlements and boundaries and all the petty concerns of mortal man, but of the intentions of the Creator, worked out over the rolling centuries, and the rise and fall of empires.

Even my uncles, obsessed as they were by Temple power games and Palace politics, recognized that Isaiah's authority was rooted in an interpretation of the world beyond their comprehension. Privately, they disliked and feared him, while publicly paying him homage, but now when I look back, I realize that they, like everyone else, relied subconsciously on his towering strength.

The night before I was taken to the Palace, my Aunt Leah created a small but painful scene which I remember only because of what happened later. Aunt Leah was my mother's younger sister. No man had married her, and she was supported by the two priest uncles; she divided her time between weaving religious tokens for them to wear about their robes, and finding fault with us children. One thing she had never learnt was that although my mother grumbled loudly and cheerfully about my father all day long when he was alive, she instantly flew into a protective rage every time Aunt Leah tried to curry favour by finding fault with him too. Aunt Leah had done more weeping and wailing about my father in the days since my return than anyone else in the household, my mother included, and liked to get me in corners to tell me what a wonderful father I had lost.

That evening, Joel asked if he could take Adad out into the city next day and describe the sights to him. The family procession to the Temple had been the first opportunity for either of them to escape from the claustrophobic tensions of the overcrowded house, and it had been a welcome diversion.

'Adad mustn't go,' said my mother at once. 'But you could go with the women when they fetch water, if you like.'

'Why can't Adad go?' asked Rebecca.

'Oh, reasons,' said my mother, and Hannah whispered to Rebecca to be quiet. Joel, though, was feeling in a provocative mood.

'It's not because he's blind, is it?' he said. 'I saw a blind man on the street today. You remember,' he added, turning to Aunt Leah, 'he asked you for money and you pushed him away. It's because he's an Assyrian, isn't it?'

All the family knew by now that Adad was an Assyrian, but nobody had said it openly. In the awkward silence that followed, everybody glanced furtively around to see if Adad was listening.

'It's all right,' said Joel loudly, his demon thoroughly roused. 'He's gone to lie down with Bathsheba. He always does that when his eye hurts. Bathsheba doesn't mind about him being an Assyrian.'

'That's because she's a brute beast, and doesn't know that all Assyrians are the cursed of Jehovah,' said Aunt Leah.

'I'll thank you to keep a civil tongue in your head about a guest in our house,' said my mother sharply. 'Besides, he was commended to us by Shear-jashub.' If my mother had hoped to silence her sister by invoking my father's name, she was mistaken.

'Was he?' said Leah. 'Was he? How do we know? Tell me that.' She turned to me. 'Your father was dead when you found him. What makes you think he intended to saddle his family for ever with an enemy upon whom the curse of Jehovah rests?'

I fumbled for some sort of answer, but it sounded unconvincing even in my own ears. Aunt Leah and I did not speak the same language, just as Aunt Leah and my father had never spoken the same language.

My uncle Shebna looked over from the men's end of the room, and took command. 'There is much justification for

Leah's point of view,' he announced ponderously. 'There have been many times in our history when Jehovah has ordained that we should kill man, woman and child without mercy, that his name be glorified; and terrible punishments have fallen upon our people who have tried to escape God's ordinance in this matter.'

'You're not going to kill Adad,' said Joel.

'That boy needs a good thrashing,' remarked Aunt Leah, and Hannah grabbed both her children and hurried them out of the room.

Uncle Shebna got up and came over to us. 'This matter is something to which I have been giving my consideration,' he said. 'What if the Lord our God has turned his face away from this city in its hour of need because he is angry that, even as we pray to him to deliver us out of the hands of the Assyrian, we are nursing one of the hated race in our bosom?'

'Exactly,' said Aunt Leah. 'He demands of us a sacrifice; he is not satisfied with the blood of bulls and goats; he. . . .'

Uncle Shebna looked at her quellingly. 'We are not like the back-sliding cult priests of the High Places,' he said. 'King Hezekiah has not pulled down the shrine at Beersheba and Lachish and Libnah in order to purify our worship, only to see their abominable practices brought back to the Great Temple itself. I hope you are not suggesting that human sacrifice is pleasing to the Lord?'

Aunt Leah was in a dilemma. 'Of course you are right, brother,' she said. 'I did not mean that the Blind One should be burnt upon the High Altar. But the death of such a one by other means would surely help to purge our sins from before the face of the Lord? We are in desperate circumstances. . . .'

'There would be more to eat without him,' one of my sisters unwisely remarked, and gave my mother a chance to take over.

'I never expected to live to hear one of my own family speak so of one to whom we are bound by the law of hospitality,' she said, and caught my sister a smart blow across the head. Having established her audience by her own means, she then turned upon her relations. 'Are you the owner of this house, Shebna? Are you, Leah? Is my husband scarcely cold in his grave before you think to take over all that is his? May the Lord prosper my enemies if I do not take a complaint about your behaviour to my husband's father. Let the prophet Isaiah stand here and tell you what he thinks of your proposals for winning the favour of Jehovah.' The likelihood of Isaiah coming down off his mountain to intervene in a domestic squabble must have appeared questionable to her even as the words left her mouth, for after a brief pause she changed tack with masterly aplomb. 'And who do you think is master in this house here and now? You, Shebna? Your brother Joah? Shear-jashub has not left me a poor unprotected woman to be ruled by her brothers. His son stands before you, tried and proved as a man, and ready to assume the government of this household. Tell them, Benjamin, what your decision is in the matter of the Blind One, Adad the Assyrian.'

I had been listening with open-mouthed enjoyment to the sound of my mother turning the full tide of her eloquence upon her own relations, and it was with something of a shock that I suddenly realized she had set me squarely in the forefront of the battle.

I had been sitting on the floor among the women and children. Now I got up and, more to give myself time to think than anything else, I strolled across and took up my position beside Uncle Shebna. He looked down at me like a comfortable fat cat asked to share its quarters with a half-grown stray and I knew I was not ready to take him on. I stared down loftily, therefore, at my Aunt Leah, noting the dull red flush creeping up from her neck, and the thin set lips.

'You know very well that my grandfather the prophet has foretold for many years that the Assyrian army will come and destroy Jerusalem. And why? Not because his son and his grandson have shown mercy to the Blind One, but because the people of the Holy City have called evil good, and good evil; and have put darkness for light, and light for darkness; and have put bitter for sweet, and sweet for bitter; they have justified the wicked for a reward, and taken away the righteousness of the righteous from him.' I paused to take a shaky breath, wondering how many more appropriate passages I could call to mind. Then I saw my mother nod slightly and I knew I had said enough to prove her point. To flounder on would be a mistake. 'Adad stays in this house,' I said, and turning away, went and took my place among the old men and male cousins at the far end of the room.

'Very good, Benjamin,' Uncle Shebna called after me. 'I can see you will make an excellent preacher one of these days.' His voice was oiled with condescension.

Next morning my two uncles escorted me to my audience with the King. I had, of course, seen Hezekiah many times before when he had come to do sacrifice at the Temple, but I had only once been inside the Palace, some years ago, when the King had thrown a great feast to celebrate the completion of the water system and all the priestly families had been invited. On that occasion Hezekiah, on being told I was Isaiah's grandson, had patted me on the head and given me grapes to eat, and told me I would live to bless the day when water flowed into the Pool of Siloam, whatever my grandfather might say.

My recollection was of a series of vast rooms panelled in carved cedar wood inlaid with ivory and mother-of-pearl, of gold and silver ornaments, and splendid statues, the whole illuminated by hundreds upon hundreds of branched oil lamps of beaten copper and silver, and in the midst, the awe-inspiring figure of the great King, robed in glorious colours and sparkling with jewels. Today, the rooms seemed just as big, but bare and dilapidated, the walls pock-marked where the decorations had been torn from their fixtures, loaded on pack-animals and sent down the winding road to Lachish behind the Rabshakeh in a last bid to buy off the Assyrian King.

In the throne room, a group of officials were gathered in earnest conversation, but the throne itself was empty. A servant went up and spoke to one of the throng, and he turned to greet us. As both my uncles bowed low before him, it dawned on me that this harassed man with a greying beard was, indeed, King Hezekiah himself. It was not just that he seemed to have shrunk physically, an impression which my own extra height would have given me, for now I stood level with him; he looked so ordinary, so human, so lacking in regal stature.

I bowed and stood waiting with downcast eyes while my Uncle Shebna explained why we had come. I was about to begin my story when a smooth young man joined us and suggested that the King listen to my tale from the comfort of his throne. As Hezekiah seated himself on the huge unadorned chair perched on its dais, Uncle Shebna told me that the young man was the King's counsellor, Eliakim. No doubt he felt that by ensuring I spoke to the King from below the dais, he was putting our mission in its proper place; but for me, the contrast between this anxious man leaning out of his vast and naked throne and the terrifying magnificence of Sennacherib emboldened rather than intimidated me.

Hezekiah listened to all I had to say resignedly, but without surprise. When I had finished, he turned to my uncles. 'You know, of course, that Sennacherib has now moved from Lachish and is making an assault on Libnah?' I suspected from the slight pause that my uncles did not know, but did not want to appear less well informed than Eliakim.

'So rumour has it,' remarked Shebna gravely.

'It is more than rumour,' said Eliakim. 'And the Rabshakeh is on his way back to Jerusalem with an army of ten thousand or so.'

'He would have brought more if he intended to attack,' remarked Joah quickly, suggesting he had been weighing up this information.

'He would not be coming at all if Sennacherib were

satisfied with our tribute,' said Eliakim. 'He will demand our surrender, and if we do not give it, he will sit at our gate and wait until Libnah has fallen and the rest of the army is free to join him.'

The three of them fell silent, waiting for Hezekiah to speak. He passed his hand wearily across his face, and turned to me.

'Where is your grandfather?' he said.

'I do not know, Sire.'

'I am surrounded by so-called advisers who hang about me with tales of woe from dawn to dusk; but the one man whom the nation needs, hides himself.'

Eliakim spoke. 'He has always prophesied that the Lord would send the Assyrians to destroy us. What can he do now, except flee to a safe place before the lightning strikes?'

'What safe place?' asked Joah. 'Samaria has fallen, Phoenicia and Philistia are in the hands of the Assyrians; all our fenced cities are taken, save only Libnah and Jerusalem, and Libnah cannot hold out long. Do you suppose, if there were any safe place, Jerusalem would be packed tight as a corn-sack with refugees?'

'Perhaps he has taken refuge in the caves above the Dead Sea,' observed Shebna, 'or crossed to the mountains of Moab. He is a man used to hardship and can survive where other men would die.'

The conversation seemed to me futile and absurd. I raised my eyes and they met Hezekiah's resting upon me. I do not think it was deliberate; he was simply withdrawing himself from these wearisome and familiar counsellors, but I was emboldened to speak.

'Isaiah will not have fled anywhere,' I said. My Uncle Shebna began to apologise for my having spoken unasked in that august company, but Hezekiah waved him into silence. His eyes showed a faint spark of interest.

'Do you think you can find him?'

'Thy servant can try.'

Uncle Shebna said, 'My brother and I will take the boy,

and a train of servants, and such offerings of oil and wine and fine wheat flour as your Majesty can yet spare from the Lord's House. . . .'

Hezekiah suddenly flared into anger, as a man will do when he has borne frustration long enough. 'When I send you and your fellow-priests to speak to Isaiah,' he said, 'it will be in sackcloth and ashes and with your clothes rent in atonement for the sins of our people. Isaiah is not one of your fat priests to be bribed with food and drink.' His eyes passed contemptuously over the priest's portly frame. 'The boy will go alone, and when he has found him, he will bring me word. Take this.' He handed me a bronze disc, stamped with the royal insignia. 'You may need it to pass our sentries.'

'How long shall I remain looking for him? What if I cannot find him?'

'Go on looking until you learn that Sennacherib is sitting upon this throne, and these priests have been hewn to pieces on their own altar as a sacrifice to the gods of the Assyrians.'

We turned and left the Palace, I proud yet fearful of the task entrusted to me, my uncles understandably sobered by the prospect Hezekiah had held out to them.

On our way home, we were overtaken by little Joel, tearing through the streets quite alone, panting and sobbing. When he saw me, he rushed up and seized me by the hand.

'Come quick,' he gasped. 'They are stoning Adad down by the Pool of Siloam.'

Chapter 8

I turned to run towards the Pool and Joel started to come with me. 'Go home, and tell my mother to send servants,' I said, for I knew he would only hold me up.

As I raced down the narrow alleys, dodging or leaping over the encampments of refugees, I kept asking myself what on earth Adad was doing down at the wall. I had heard Joel's request the previous night, and my mother's uncompromising refusal, and I had just got around to thinking about Aunt Leah's outburst when I nearly bumped into her. She was walking fast away from the Pool, holding her shawl across the lower part of her face, so I could not see her expression but I noted her bright eyes and flushed forehead. An inkling of the truth began to dawn.

I could hear the hoarse cries of men engaged in cruel sport, and the screams of women egging them on, long before I reached the Pool. Then I came in sight of the pulsating mob gathered like a swarm of bees around the steps surrounding the water. Those behind were shoving and shouting, and some, armed with cobble-stones, were trying to force their way through; while others, turning back to look for missiles, tried to grab them from the hands of those who had them already. From above, I could see Adad, like a bear in a pit, crouched against the back wall, his arms folded across his eyes, while the encircling tormentors stamped and shouted.

Only two things had saved him from serious injury or death—the lack of convenient stones, and the cramped nature of the place. Men were fighting among themselves for stones, and when they could push their way through to the front of the crowd, the press of people all around prevented them from throwing accurately or with sufficient violence most of the time, though now and again a missile found its mark and as Adad flinched the crowd raised a shrill clamour of triumph.

Just for a moment, the possibility of walking away crossed my mind. It was anger, not courage, that drove me, kicking, striking and biting through the hate-inflamed mob. Burning behind my eyes I saw the vindictive self-righteous face of Aunt Leah, tripping home to claim Jehovah's congratulations; but the image was no more than a single stone loosened from the dam built to retain the flood-waters and now crumbling after a storm. All the deaths and injuries and cruelties, all the hatred and unnecessary miseries that this war had unleashed upon my world, seemed to come boiling up from the depths of my very soul, and drove me, screaming with rage like a madman, into the human cage where Adad crouched alone.

For one moment, my sudden eruption into the scene produced a hush of surprise. I was dressed quite literally fit for a king and in my richly dyed robe and embroidered head covering I might almost have carried enough authority to halt the slaughter, had I not tripped over my own unaccustomed ankle-length garment and tumbled ignominiously down the last few steps.

There was some laughter, and one man cried, 'Out of the way, laddie.' I scrambled to my feet and, with what dignity I could muster, called upon the crowd to disperse, but my words passed unheard by all but a few, and those few responded with angry cries. In a moment, the whole mob were baying like hounds, and the stones began to fly once more. One hit me on the cheekbone and only then did it come home to me that I faced death, here and now, in this trap, and at the hands of my own countrymen.

I glanced round for a way of escape, and realized that

Adad himself stood right by the mouth of the tunnel that brought the water all the way from the Gihon spring outside the city walls—Hezekiah's famous engineering feat. After the rains, the water bubbled up above the level of the entrance, but by this time of year the outflow barely reached half-way up the tunnel mouth.

I grasped Adad by the shoulder. 'Quick!' I shouted. 'Hold on to me!' I ducked down into the hole, and turned to force Adad's head down, too, explaining what I was doing as well as I could. He seemed to understand, and came stumbling and splashing after me, until I was brought up short by the enveloping blackness.

'Go on, go on, I'm all right,' urged Adad, pressing forward. 'They will come after us.'

Indeed, looking back, I could see figures outlined against the sun-bright entrance, and heard splashing water nearer at hand than the muffled cries of the mob.

'I can't hurry,' I said. 'It's pitch dark.'

Adad, amazingly, laughed softly. 'Then let me lead,' he said. 'I'm rather good in the dark.'

A stone came ricocheting down the tunnel as we squeezed past each other between the narrow walls, but it fell harmlessly a few paces short of us. I gripped Adad's tunic and, with head tucked well down, scuttled blindly after him at what seemed to me a breakneck pace, knee-deep in water. Then the water grew deeper, and soon it was swirling round our waists. I began to worry lest roof and water surface should meet, but just then Adad paused, and said, 'You can stand now.'

I straightened my aching back, and put my hand up to feel for the roof, but met only empty space.

'How do you know . . .?' I began, but he interrupted me.

'Ssh! Keep still. Listen!' We held our breath, but the only sound to reach our ears was the steady drip of water from condensation gathering on the rock walls. The blackness was absolute; not even a pinprick of light showed from either entrance.

Adad let out a shuddering sigh. He had acted quickly and coolly when I had come to his rescue, but now the terror began to catch up with him.

'It's all right,' I said. 'Nobody is following us.'

'What about the other end?'

'I . . . I don't know. It's outside the walls. I don't *think* they'll go round. There's guards on all the gates for one thing.'

'They could get torches and come after us. They could come from both ends. They could trap us in the middle.' He was shaking violently, and I had tasted briefly enough of the terror he must have endured to feel a trembling in my own limbs, but it may have been due to the cold water.

'Let's go along a bit,' I said. 'I think there's a place where we can get up on a ledge, out of the water.'

'I don't know . . .' he said confusedly, and seemed to dither about as though he did not know which way to go. I had an anxious feeling that he was about to pass out.

'This way,' I said loudly in his ear, and grasping him firmly under the armpits, propelled him onwards into the blackness.

Luckily we had not far to go, for he was barely conscious and I, hampered by my long sodden robe and with Adad's weight on my arms, was near collapse, when with a startled cry Adad fell forward on to his face. Instead of subsiding into the waist-deep water, however, he had fallen forward on to a ledge over which the stream barely trickled. This was the place I had in mind, for once, when the tunnel was first completed, I had been through it, as had just about every inhabitant of Jerusalem, in great parties with oil lamps, all exclaiming at the wonderful achievement. Here, in the very centre of Mount Ophel, thirty metres below ground, the two work parties hacking their way through from either end had miraculously met. Not with absolute exactitude, however; indeed, the wonder was that they had met at all, and had it not been that each party had heard voices, they might have passed each other by, tunnelling away in parallel, two paces apart. As a result, there was a sharply-angled turn where the two passages joined, and a sudden change in level. Later the passage had been widened somewhat to smooth out the angle, but the shelf of rock remained. The water flowed in a shallow trickle at this time of year from the Gihon end, but where the bottom fell away it filled up to the depth we had been wading through. Feeling about me in the darkness I found a wide dry shelf to the side of the stream—no doubt under water in the rainy season—and coaxed and heaved Adad up on to it.

'We can rest here,' I said. 'It's safe enough.'

There is a kind of false familiarity in dealing with the blind. Sighted people only use their hands to touch those whom they know and love, apart from the rituals of greeting. Blind people have to use their hands as we use our eyes, to find out whereabouts and dimensions if they are not to live in a vacuum. I sensed how Adad shrank from this personal contact with strangers and enemies, and knew I would feel the same way myself. He seldom felt for me if he needed help, for fear of seeming to show over-familiarity, but held out his hand for me to take; that way, our two hands were like tools, empty of feelings. The only time I remember him touching my face was when he rose up in rage and nearly throttled me.

Now, as I knelt by him, trying to make sure in the blackness that he was securely lodged, his hands came up and grasped me by the shoulders.

'Benjamin,' he said, 'you are the best friend I have ever had. I wish I could see your face.' There was such unfeigned feeling in his voice that I could not help but be moved.

'You can see it as well as I can see yours at the moment,' I said, boyish, a little embarrassed, but I took his right hand from my shoulder and guided it to my face. The fingers travelled lightly over my features, feeling the angle of bone and curve of hair-line; I flinched a little as they passed over the bruise caused by a flying stone. Then he leant forward and hugged me in the double embrace which is the common form of greeting between Jew and Jew, and between Assyrian and Assyrian, but never between Assyrian and Jew.

'I think there must be one God only,' he said. 'Whether he is your God or my God, I do not know; but how can there be one God who loves you and hates me, and one God who hates you and loves me?'

I returned his embrace, deeply moved, but left the question unanswered; it struck me that, with my upbringing, I knew too much about theology and too little about God.

It was not exactly cold in the tunnel, but the air was dank, and we, of course, were both wet through. It would not be safe to try and return the way we had come until nightfall, and even then it would be risky; besides, it was now scarcely midday, and the thought of sitting there long in our sodden clothes in the dark and chill was unendurable. The answer seemed to be to press on to the Gihon entrance, though I could not believe that, at such a time as this, it would be neither barred nor guarded. Still, at least we could go and investigate.

Adad had suffered a few more bruises than I, mainly on his arms, but he was not seriously injured, and had managed to protect his face. Even so, he was reluctant to move, although shaken intermittently with violent shivering fits; like a hunted fox who has gone to earth, it was as though he had found a refuge from all the problems of life. Even his aching loneliness had been eased by opening his heart to me, and he was in a mood in which he was content to curl up and die where he lay.

He was, however, as docile as when I first came upon him nursing my father, and when I told him my plan he meekly followed me down the tunnel.

The going was much easier now, because the water was barely above our ankles, and before long I saw a pinprick of light ahead of me. As we got nearer, I saw I was right about one thing; there were bars across the entrance.

I told Adad to wait, and crept up to take a closer look. At least, if it was barred, there was less likelihood of an armed guard posted there, and peering out, I could detect no sign of one. I studied the bars carefully, wondering if it were possible to squeeze between them—it might be for me, but I was sure Adad would be too broad-shouldered. I went back and told him what I had discovered. He had revived somewhat, and came to me to examine the problem for himself. Having felt the gaps between the bars, he explored the area above, testing the overhanging rock, and then underneath.

'There's no room there,' I said, for the space was barely a handsbreadth.

'Lot of silt,' he said, burrowing away with his hands.

I joined in, and as we cleared away the pebbles and other debris, a couple of boulders began to emerge, which were not part of the rock floor of the tunnel. It became evident that when the bars had been fixed, the workmen had pushed the boulders up against them on the inside, where no would-be infiltrator could get at them. The thought that someone might want to get out, rather than in, had not concerned them. We worked away, and eventually were able to shift the two big stones and push them further up the tunnel. The space they revealed was not very big, but would be enough, provided one was prepared to sidle through with one's face under water.

I didn't much like the prospect of doing it, for fear of getting stuck and drowning like a rat in a pipe, but it must have been worse for Adad, because not only was he bigger, but he could not see what he was being asked to do. However, he felt very carefully round the edges of the aperture, and declared himself ready to try. I went first, partly because I was smaller, but also so that, once out, I could take a good look to make sure no one was watching us. It was all clear in the valley below and, as I already knew, the sheer rock face above the tunnel entrance shielded us from the city walls, so Adad pushed through the bundle of my unsuitable bulky robe, which I had taken off, and then squeezed through after me.

We stood, wet through and cold in the shadow of the ravine, but across on the slopes of the Mount of Olives the sun was shining with a brilliance that dazzled me after the total darkness of the tunnel. I could see a group of women coming up the track, carrying water pots, which made me aware that although the city dwellers no longer used the Gihon spring for their regular water supply, preferring the more convenient Pool of Siloam, it was still the local well for the scatter of people who lived outside the walls, and the nomadic tribesmen who wandered the neighbouring hills with their flocks. There was no reason to fear the women, but I realized we must look a curious pair, the blind and foreign-sounding Adad and I in my soiled and sodden splendid robe.

During the last few days, living in the claustrophobic huddle of ill-fed refugees, I suppose I had acquired a siege mentality, because it surprised me to find *anyone* quietly going about their business outside the city walls; but as I looked around, I saw there were quite a lot of people about. Some were chopping wood in the olive groves, some were scavenging, face to the parched earth, for whatever could be eaten or burnt. In the distance, high on a hill-top to the right, I thought I could even detect a flock of goats on the move. Life, I realized, does not stop when war threatens; it goes on, as best it can, until death strikes. Nevertheless, the valley was unusually quiet, because there were no children playing. In ordinary times, the Kidron valley was a favourite resort for groups of girls to saunter and giggle, and young boys to play wild games among the rocks and trees, but now the only people to venture out of the protection of the city walls were those whom necessity drove out by day, to return each night.

'We'll get into the sunshine,' I said, and we clambered down into the stream bed and up into the olive groves opposite, as I had done all those years ago when I joined my grandfather watching the building of the tunnel. Once again, I wanted to find Isaiah, but this time it was more important and likely to be more difficult. I explained my mission to Adad, and persuaded him that he would be safe and warm lying out in the sun, on the westward-facing slope in a clearing among trees, while I went home to change into more suitable clothes for my undertaking. Adad's thin cotton tunic would dry soon enough in that hot sun, but my cumbersome robe hung heavy and clammy on me; besides, although I felt too angry with most of my family to want to speak to them, I did not wish to take off on what could be a dangerous mission into the mountains without a word to my mother, or to little Joel, whose prompt action had saved Adad from a horrible death.

I asked Adad how he had come to be there, by the Pool, and his explanation fitted pretty well with my suspicions.

'It was your Aunt Leah,' he said. 'She suddenly asked if I would like to accompany her, because Joel had told her I was interested in the buildings. I said no, at first, because . . . well, it wasn't exactly that I didn't trust her, but she had never seemed to like me particularly, and I was a bit surprised. Then I thought perhaps I'd got two of your aunts confused. You've got such a big family, and they all talk alike, and when you can't see them, it's difficult to be sure; and then she said Joel wanted to come too, but he wouldn't come without me. Anyway, I *did* want to get out, and I wanted to please Hannah, because she's always been so good to me, and I thought she'd be glad for Joel to get out for a bit—you know how moody he gets with all that crowd in the courtyard all the time—so I said yes.'

'And then?'

'It was all right at first. Joel kept asking questions about the different places, and she told him things—you know, a bit like a teacher—and then we came to the well. She told me some tale about how if I went down the steps to the water, and bathed my eye, there might be a miracle. She sounded all tight and high in her voice, and I felt her hand trembling as she almost pushed me along ahead of her, and I thought perhaps she is some sort of priestess going into a trance. It was frightening—there were so many people all round, and I knew there was this pool somewhere, and I thought I was going to fall on the steps. And then I realized she had left go of me, and she must have pulled Joel away with her, because I felt round with my hands and touched some stranger, who shook me off like a beggar.

'Then suddenly I heard her screaming." The Blind One is sent by God to be a curse to us! He is the enemy—he is the Assyrian. Jehovah is angry that we have allowed an Assyrian to be alive in our city; that is why the city is to be destroyed; that is why your bellies are empty and your little children are dying. . . ." I don't remember all of it. She kept shouting the same things over and over again. At first, people didn't hear her, because of the noise; but then they hushed, and were quite silent, while she screamed on and on, about how I was accursed, and brought God's curse upon Jerusalem, and how I must be killed that the city might be saved. Then there was a sound like a dog makes before it begins to bark—you know, a sort of low growling in its throat—and then they all began to shout and scream, with her voice still shrill over all—and then the first stone hit the wall behind me. After that the stones kept coming, and there was no way I could turn . . . I tried to pray to my gods, or to your God, to save me, but all I kept thinking was, "Where's Benjamin . . .?" and suddenly, you were there.' He shook his head, and asked, as if the thought had only just occurred to him, 'How did you come to be there?'

'Joel told me,' I said, and explained how we had met him. 'He must have taken a wrong turn to be where he was,' I added. 'God cannot mean you to die.'

I left Adad lying on the sun-baked ground in the clearing I had remembered. It was so hot that I thought, wet as he was, he should at least make sure his head was in the shade.

'Yes,' he said. 'I will in a little while.' He was cocking his face up sideways at the sun, and spoke absently.

'You don't want to give yourself a headache,' I said.

'No, mother,' he replied, with a sudden grin. He seemed extraordinarily cheerful, all things considered.

I ran back down the slope, aiming north of the Gihon tunnel towards the Great Gate and the steps that led directly up to the Temple. I wanted to avoid the gateway further south, which would bring me uncomfortably close to the Pool of Siloam, but as I approached the entrance I realized the whole Temple Mount was swarming with people. It was the time for the King's daily sacrifice, but obviously this was an especially important one, as just about the entire male population of Jerusalem appeared to be packed into the surrounding courtyard. Presumably Hezekiah was making a last desperate effort to appease the wrath of Jehovah before the arrival of the Rabshakeh. No doubt the men who that morning had been hurling stones at a blind youth and a priest's son were now importuning the Lord to spare them.

I was in no state to make myself conspicuous in such a throng, so I circled right round to the north and came in by the Fish Gate. Of course there were guards on the gate, but I held Hezekiah's token and was allowed to pass without question. The streets were deserted, except for the workmen still trying to complete the new north wall; all the other men were at the Temple, and the women and children were praying in their houses, if they had them; they had flocked to watch King Hezekiah pass and share in the ceremonies from the outskirts.

The first person I saw as I entered our courtyard was Aunt Leah, standing in an attitude of prayer. All the women were there, but it was only Aunt Leah that I noticed. She was loudly reciting penitential psalms, and beating her breast, but she stopped dead when she saw me. All the others fell silent too, and watched me, waiting.

Clothed in cold anger, I walked past, wordlessly. In the doorway, I brushed past my mother, who made an exclamation as she put out her hand and felt the state of my robe. Ignoring her, I went to the clothes chest, threw off my wet clothes, rubbed myself with a towel, and with leisurely dignity selected a good strong workaday tunic and put it on. Then I washed my hands and face in the ewer of water. I knew my mother had followed me and was standing in the doorway, but I would not acknowledge even her presence with so much as a glance. This frozen rage with my entire family made everything quite easy, so long as I allowed no member of it to breach my defences.

Then there was a child's cry, and Rebecca came running in and clung to me.

'Where is Adad?' she cried. 'Is he hurt? Joel told me. . . .' Beyond my mother, I could see Joel's pale face, and I knew I could not leave without a word.

'Adad is all right,' I said. 'Now I must find my grandfather.'

My mother nodded. No doubt the uncles had related all that part of the morning's events. I had expected a torrent of words from her, whether of anger, or support, or fear, I did not know; but I found her silence more moving than all her volubility. I knelt before her, as I would have for a blessing from my father.

'May the Lord bless and keep you, and all you hold dear,' she said. Then she lifted me up, and kissed me on both cheeks.

I dared not speak, for I would not pass that mob in the courtyard with tears in my eyes. I took her hands between my own, then turned and walked away through the silent courtyard. I felt Aunt Leah's burning eyes upon me, but I would not look at her.

Chapter 9

As I emerged from our gate, I could see the sacrifice was over, and the departing crowds were pouring out from the Temple Courtyard. I had no wish to meet my uncles, so turned away and left Jerusalem by the way I had entered. Just before I reached the Fish Gate, two soldiers went running past me; others were gathering on the walls, staring out to the northern approaches.

'The Assyrians are coming!' was the word everywhere.

I climbed up to the parapet, remembering vividly that morning in Lachish when we had all first set eyes on Sennacherib's war-machine. Now I was a hardened campaigner, and coolly assessed the size of the oncoming force, and its distance away. I guessed it was not the whole army, but the Rabshakeh at the head of his ten thousand, come to demand surrender, not to attack.

The guards looked at me a little oddly as I presented my pass and walked out through the gate—everybody was coming in, the foragers and scavengers whom I had seen before, and the few families who still lived outside the city. My only real worry was that Adad might have taken fright at the sound of the oncoming force, and stumbled away into some sheltered corner, but I need not have feared. The tramp of horses' hoofs and jingle of harness did not carry to the tree-fringed oasis where I had left him. True, he was standing, alert and listening, but not to the sound of armies on the move.

'It's me, Benjamin,' I said, to reassure him.

'Listen!' he whispered.

'It's the Assyrian force,' I began, although I could hear nothing.

'No, not that.' He stood with his head cocked towards the hill, his hand outstretched to me to signify stillness, but all I could hear was the rustle of olive leaves and the distant cry of a hoopoe. He seemed, not frightened, but strangely elated.

'*He* was here,' he whispered.

'Who?'

'The messenger of God; the Great One who knows all things.'

'My grandfather? Isaiah?'

'I know not. But he knew me. He knows all things. He walks with God.'

It is hard to get excited about someone you have known all your life, proud though I was of the reputation of my grandfather, but I could think of no one else likely to make such an impression on Adad. If he had truly spoken with Isaiah, my task looked like being easily accomplished—and just as well, too, with the Rabshakeh at the gates, demanding his answer.

'What did he look like, this Man of God?' I asked, forgetting, but Adad seemed not to notice.

'Tall,' he said. 'Eyes like coals of fire. Shining like silver; with wings, with wings. He touched my eyes with a dazzling, and he said I should see again.'

'And can you?'

'Yes, yes! No. Not *now*. But I saw *him*. I saw him in my soul!'

My first thought was that too much had befallen Adad, and he had lost his wits and gained in their place the gift of ecstasy, or second sight. Then it struck me that maybe he had simply been too much in the hot sun. Whatever miracle he thought Isaiah had performed, he clearly could not see now, any more than before, and I knew my grandfather had little use for wonder-workers, and had never sought to be one.

'What do you mean, he said you should see?' I asked, cautiously.

'I had fallen asleep, I think, and I woke to the sound of his voice. "Whom shall he teach knowledge?" he was saying. "And whom shall he make to understand? Them that are weaned from the milk, and drawn from the breasts." No. There was something before that, about priests who have eaten and drunk, and err in vision, and stumble in judgement. And then he said, "Nay, but by men of strange lips and another tongue will he speak to this people." You see, he knew I was a foreigner, even though I had not spoken.'

'Maybe,' I said cautiously, 'he didn't actually notice you were here. When he talks with God, he does not know much of what goes on around him.'

'I spoke to him, and he answered. I said, "I am a man of strange lips and of another tongue." He said, "So therefore you shall lay in Judah a foundation stone, a tried stone, a precious corner stone." He spoke of all the tools of the architect, the measuring rule, and the plummet line. I said, "How can a blind man be a builder?" Then, then he said it.'

'Said what?'

'He lifted me up from the ground—I think I had been kneeling—and faced me to the sun, and said, "The wisdom of wise men shall vanish, and the understanding of prudent men shall be lost; but in that day the deaf shall hear when a book is read, and the eyes of the blind shall see out of the impenetrable darkness." Out of the impenetrable darkness,' he repeated, his voice vibrant with longing.

I was silent. What could I say? My grandfather had been saying things like that for decades. Was it chance, or deliberate intent, or the unguessed purpose of Jehovah, that he had spoken them in Adad's hearing?

'When did he leave you?' I asked, after a suitably reverent pause. I had my task to perform.

'Not long before you came, I think. I heard his voice going away and away, up the hill.'

'*Up* the hill?'

'Why yes. That was where he told me you would find him.'

'He mentioned *me* to you?'

'He said, "Tell the son of my dead son, whom Hezekiah has sent to find me, to seek the Word of the Lord where the East looks upon the West, and the North looks upon the South."'

'And that means the top of the hill?'

'I suppose so, don't you? I mean, it makes sense.'

I shook my head in bewilderment. I just couldn't make it out at all. All I could guess at was that there had been a meeting between two people both poised on the trembling whisker point between two worlds, each understanding the other, whether caught up in the spirit or set down upon the earth.

How did Isaiah know the link between Adad and me? How had he heard of my father's death? How did he know I was on Hezekiah's mission? And if he knew all this, then he must have chosen his words to Adad consciously. Was he really foretelling that Adad would get his sight back, and follow his chosen calling as an architect?

'Come on,' I said. 'We'll go and look for him.'

Unexpectedly, Adad shook his head. 'You go,' he said. 'It is your business. The Messenger of God has already spoken to me. He has no more to say to me.'

'Are you sure?' I asked. It would be much quicker and easier to catch up with my grandfather by myself. 'Will you be safe? The Assyrian force is approaching Jerusalem from the north.'

'I shall be safe,' said Adad. 'Nothing can happen to harm me now.'

Such a remark struck me as tempting providence, but Adad was wrapped in spiritual armour.

I toiled up to the top of the hill, pausing to look back to check the progress of the Assyrian force. The entire army appeared to be mounted, and was settling down in a great encampment on the high ground of the city, so far as I could see, although a number of detachments had separated off and were reconnoitring the city approaches. One large group was trotting along the lower slope of the Mount of Olives, below the grove, and just above the steep incline running down to the Kidron. I hoped none of them would penetrate into the trees and discover Adad, but their attention appeared to be directed solely towards the city.

I found Grandfather Isaiah, as he had said, on the very top of the hill. He stood with one arm flung out to the north, uttering incantations, presumably about the conquered people of Samaria, or their Assyrian overlords, because next he turned and pointed west, straight over my head, and as I approached I could hear him pronouncing doom upon the gods of the countries that lay between Judah and the sea, Phoenicia and Philistia. Ignoring me completely as I panted up the last few paces, he turned again and hurled a series of derisory comments in the general direction of Egypt, that powerful southern neighbour whom he had so often warned Hezekiah not to trust for aid; and then, shifting once again, till the afternoon sun shone on his left cheek, he called up the dark princes of Ethiopia, that mysterious and far-flung land, to be tools in the hands of Jehovah to bring about the downfall of Assyria.

Then, without turning or showing the slightest sign of being aware of my presence, he said, 'I tell you that as birds fly, so will the Lord of Hosts protect Jerusalem. Then shall fall the Assyrian, but not with the sword of man. And tell your friend that my people shall dwell in a peaceable habitation, and in sure dwellings, and in quiet resting places. And tell that priest, Shebna, the Treasurer, that the Lord will hurl him away violently; he shall surely turn and toss him like a ball in a large country; and Eliakim, the son of Hilkiah, that I will fasten him like a nail in a sure place, and they shall hang upon him all the glory of his father's house; but in that day, the nail will be hewn down, and fall. Tell them,' he added, suddenly turning round and looking down at me, 'to meet me upon the bottom step of the Temple at sunset, to take my message to Hezekiah.'

'Did you know,' I said hesitantly, 'that your son that was my father, is dead?'

'Shear-jashub; a remnant shall remain.' He showed no sign of surprise. 'Oh, Judah, your country is desolate; your cities are burned with fire; your land, strangers devour it in your presence and it is desolate; and the daughter of Zion is left as a cottage in a vineyard, as a shed in a garden of cucumbers, as a besieged city. Except the Lord of Hosts had left us a very small remnant, we should have been as Sodom and Gomorrah.'

'As a shed in a garden of cucumbers,' I repeated, thinking how strange it was that he should use that image.

'You are the son of my son,' he said, suddenly looking straight at me. I knelt, and, like any grandfather, he gave me the traditional blessing. Then he said, 'You are of those that remain; in that day then shall the branch of the Lord be beautiful, and glorious, and the fruit of the earth shall be excellent for them that are escaped; and it shall come to pass that he that is left in Zion, that remaineth in Jerusalem, shall be called holy.'

I ran back down the hill as the shadows filled the trough of the Kidron, bewildered, elated and fearful. Chiefly I wondered whether the call to a state of holiness required me to pass on *all* of Isaiah's messages, word for word, or whether I could gloss over his remarks about my uncles.

Just before I slipped into the shadow of the trees, I saw that a great conclave of horsemen had gathered immediately below, opposite the Great Gate, with the valley of the Kidron between. The walls of the Temple Mount were lined with priests and all the important men of the city. On either side, as far as the limits of the eastern wall, the parapets were crammed with all the ordinary people, citizens and refugees. On my side of the brook, there was much blowing of horns and beating of cymbals, on the other, a deathly hush. The music seemed to be building up into a crescendo; then it stopped, suddenly, and in the silence I heard the voice of one man, calling across the valley.

I ran through the trees and found Adad sitting up and listening, with a strange expression on his face.

'It is I, Benjamin,' I said, as usual. 'Has anyone been here? Are you all right?'

He nodded. 'The man who is speaking,' he said, '—it is my father.'

I looked at him, trying to guess his mood.

'It is all right,' he said. 'I am not afraid. But I would like to hear what he is saying.'

That was what I wanted, too, so we made our way cautiously down towards the lower edge of the grove. It was not difficult to find cover, because juniper and myrtle bushes grew in haphazard clusters on the rocky shelves below the olives, but I had to take care that Adad was well hidden, because of course he could not see when he was exposed.

'I will give you a thousand horses,' the Rabshakeh was saying, mockingly, 'if you are able to set riders on them. How can you turn away one of the least of my master's officers, or put your trust in the chariots and horsemen of the Egyptians? Your Lord has sent me up against this land to destroy it.'

He had been speaking in the Semitic language that Adad and I both used, and which was understood by both our peoples, though the pronunciation was different; but now my Uncle Shebna, after consultation with Eliakim, whom I could see beside him, shouted out to him to use Aramaic, the language of scholars and diplomats.

The Rabshakeh laughed, and turned to the silent masses.

'Who should I speak to? These your masters, or you, who will be the first to die of slow starvation? Hear the message of the Great King of Assyria. These are the King's words. Do not be taken in by Hezekiah. He cannot save you. Do not let him persuade you to rely on your God, or that this city will never be surrendered to the King of Assyria. Come out to me, and then you shall each eat of the fruit of your own vine, and your own fig-tree, and drink the water of your own cistern, until I come and take you to a land like your own, a land of grain and new wine, of corn and vineyards. Beware lest Hezekiah mislead you by telling you that the Lord will save you. Where are the gods of Samaria? Did they save Samaria from me? Among all the gods of the nations I have conquered, is there one who saved his land from me? And how is Jehovah to save Jerusalem?'

He waited for some response from the people, but they remained silent. I learnt afterwards that the King had sent his soldiers about the city with strict orders that no one was to respond to whatever terms the Rabshakeh offered, and there were soldiers posted all along the walls to make sure the order was obeyed. I do not think they would have yielded anyhow, because they had all seen or heard of the fate of those who surrendered in the other fenced cities. All the same, Hezekiah had reason to doubt the loyalty of many of the refugees, for they had come from cities, like Beersheba and Lachish, where his actions in pulling down the local shrines had been much resented.

In the pause that followed, I turned to Adad, and asked him. 'Hearing your own father like that . . . does it make you feel you would like to go back?'

Adad shook his head. 'No,' he said. 'No. It would be terrible for him—he would have to kill me, for his own honour and the discipline of the troops. It is better as it is. He will go home thinking he has a dead hero for a son.'

'But what about you? You will have to spend the rest of your life among strangers.'

'So; I had thought death was better, but not any more; at least, not if I can see again. Without sight,' he shook his head, 'without sight, I don't suppose I shall live long anyway. If it comes to an attack on Jerusalem, like the attack on Lachish, there will be so many deaths, that one blind man is hardly likely to escape.' He put out a hand, and found my arm. 'You are a good friend, Benjamin, and have saved my life more than once, but the Assyrian army is not the same thing as a rabble round a watering-place. Then it will be every man for himself, if the remnant is to be saved.'

'Whose side are you on?' I asked, half-joking, because he had picked up Isaiah's phrase.

'No side,' he said. 'Not your uncle's, not my father's. I have found where I belong. I belong to the people in the middle—people like Hannah and Joel and Rebecca; the homeless ones. They are the ones who need a builder.'

The horsemen below us wheeled and shouted orders, and began to canter away back to their encampment to the north. The Rabshakeh would get no answer till the morning. Meanwhile, I had to get back into the city to deliver my message. Already the sun was sliding down towards the roof of the Temple, and chill shade enveloped us.

Peering out from the juniper bushes, I could see that a cluster of horsemen remained opposite the Great Gate, and looking away to my left, I could see another group positioned so as to overlook the Water and Dung Gates. It would be foolish to go round to the north to get to the Fish Gate, because that was where the main Assyrian force was encamped. There appeared to be only one possible way by which I could regain entrance to the city.

'I'll have to go back through the tunnel,' I said.

'Can you get there without being seen?'

'I think so. It's deep in a cleft, and there's quite a bit of cover on this side. What will you do? I can't be sure of getting back before nightfall.'

'Is there a shed nearby where I could lie up?'

'I should imagine so. Or an empty house. Let's go and see.'

I led Adad up through the trees and towards a small group of buildings on the southern edge of the grove. Here, to my surprise, we found an old woman milking a goat into a bowl, and, standing patiently watching, my grandfather Isaiah. He seemed to have the cat's ability to appear unexpectedly a long way from where he had last been seen, without ever being detected on the move. When the bowl was full, the woman handed it to Isaiah, with some flat barley cake, which he dipped into the warm milk, and ate in a matter-of-fact manner. I had remained silent, uncertain what to say, but after a few mouthfuls, Isaiah spoke to the woman, in ordinary everyday tones.

'Will you care for the Blind One until the boy returns?' he said. 'It may be tonight, it may not be for some days.' He handed the bowl back to her, half-empty.

'The Blind One shall stay,' she replied, 'but I, too, have a request to make.'

'Speak.'

'The Lord has not blessed this goat with good warm milk for you to look slightingly upon it. I will take the lad into my house when the bowl is empty.'

The shadow of a smile glimmered on the Prophet's austere face as he meekly took the bowl back. I hastily explained the situation to Adad, and to the old woman, though she seemed quite content to accept him as part of her service to Isaiah, and then ran off down the hill. As I wriggled down the river bank through the low scrub, and sprinted across and up to the shelter of the rock overhanging the Gihon spring, I wondered how Isaiah was going to bypass the watching Assyrians. Not, I felt sure, by the undignified route I was taking.

I had to grit my teeth to crawl in the cold water and squeeze under the bar, but once inside, the journey back through the darkness to the Pool of Siloam seemed quite short. I emerged apprehensively, clutching Hezekiah's token in case I met a hostile reception, but the only people there were three young girls with water pots, who stared at me with scared eyes.

'Peace be with you,' I remarked conversationally, and giggling nervously, they returned the greeting.

I went straight to the Palace Gate, wet and bedraggled as I was. As well as from a sense of urgency, I had no wish to encounter my uncles before delivering my message to Hezekiah. The tension of the time showed in the response of the guards, who let me through on sight of the token without hesitation or the slightest hint of amusement. I would have been less than human not to feel a spark of self-importance as, alone and unaccompanied by any of my august relations, I was passed from official to official without delay, and brought before the King himself. To my relief, although Eliakim was with him, Shebna was not, so, albeit hesitantly, I delivered the Prophet's message, word for word. Eliakim would have to take the bad with the good, and anyhow I did not have to live with him.

'Those are all the words of the Prophet?' asked the King, when I had finished.

'They are all the words to your servant, neither have I added one word nor taken one away,' I said. The sons of scribes and priests are taught to commit long passages to memory from such an early age that I could answer with a clear conscience.

'If the Lord God permits the sun to shine upon the King of Judah for many days, he will not forget the service performed by the grandson of the Prophet,' replied Hezekiah. 'How,' he added, dropping the courtly form of address, 'did you get back into the city?'

'Once, when your servant was a child, you told him that he would live to bless the day when Hezekiah's Conduit was completed.'

'You are to be congratulated on your resourcefulness,' said the King.

Eliakim interposed smoothly. 'I believe it is not once, but twice today, that the boy has made use of the King's water system.' Obviously rumours had been going the rounds of the city.

'Have I my lord's permission to go?' I asked.

'You have; but first go with this servant, who has my orders to clothe you with a tunic of fine linen, and an overgarment of the best wool.'

'I thank my lord, and pray he may prosper through many days; since my lord looks kindly upon me, may I be so bold as to make one further request?'

'Speak what you have to say.'

'Is it necessary for me to repeat the words of the Prophet in their entirety to Shebna, the Treasurer of the Lord's Temple?'

For a moment, the gravity of Hezekiah's expression lifted a little. 'No,' he said. 'That is a task we will depute to Eliakim, the son of Hilkiah.'

I was taken off, bathed and anointed and handsomely dressed, and given a good meal, thinking how strangely my encounter with the two kings complemented each other. Sennacherib had stripped me of my borrowed uniform and sent me half-naked away; now I was leaving Hezekiah's Palace clothed in royal finery.

If I had been in danger of thinking my brief royal audience was anything more than a passing diversion for the King, I soon learnt otherwise, for on my return through the Palace apartments I passed Hezekiah standing with a group of priests, Eliakim and my uncles included, all barefoot and in penitential robes. Official mourners, and servants bearing caskets of ashes, stood by; the procession to meet Isaiah was about to begin. No one paid the slightest attention to me, so I walked quickly out across the courtyard and down the steps to the street, now lined with silent waiting crowds. I waited with them and soon the solemn procession emerged, the barefoot priests uttering the sobbing rhythms of the penitential psalms, and tearing at their rough hair-cloth garments, while the servants with the caskets shook ashes over their heads, and the mourners accompanied all with loud and steady wailing, soon taken up by the waiting crowds.

As the procession moved towards the Temple, the crowds followed along behind, parting to the right and left as the priests climbed up to the raised terrace, and keeping pace with them along the lower ground till we all reached the foot of the Altar of Burnt Offering. Here the priests paused, but they did not mount up to the altar; instead they proceeded, step by step, down the stone stairs to the Great Gateway, stopping on every step to prostrate themselves on the stones, beating their foreheads in the dust, and wailing.

There was no sign of Isaiah. I began to wonder whether he had, after all, been thwarted by the presence of the Assyrian outposts, or been taken prisoner by them; or even, the thought flashed across my mind, been killed. If once the besieged Judaeans got the idea he was dead, or had abandoned them, I knew their resistance would crumble like dust. Then, suddenly, over the rolling waves of lamentation, I heard his voice, powerful, exalted, unmistakable. The wailing died away, and all heads turned towards the Temple entrance, from which the procession had just laboriously descended.

There, standing high upon the Great Altar, and framed between the two gigantic pillars behind him, stood the Prophet, arms outstretched to the sky.

'This is the word of the Lord, the God of Israel: I have heard your prayer concerning Sennacherib, King of Assyria. This is the word which the Lord has spoken concerning him: "The virgin daughter of Zion disdains you, she laughs you to scorn; the daughter of Jerusalem tosses her head as you retreat."'

Fine words, but as I looked at the despairing hungry faces round me I could not help wondering whether the great man, alone on his mountain, had not lost touch with reality. These people were not laughing anyone to scorn. Yet they listened as the powerful voice rolled on, speaking of the pride of the Assyrians, and how they boasted of having gone up with chariots into the mountains of Lebanon, and cut down the tallest of their cedars, and marched across the desert lands, drying up all the streams of Egypt; but all this was part of God's plan.

The people listened patiently, although they had heard all this before; but Isaiah's miraculous appearance and the magic of his eloquence held them spellbound.

"'I will put a ring in your nose," says our God,
"and a hook in your lips,
and I will take you back by the road
on which you have come.'"

There was a stirring among the crowd, as of a giant awakening out of a coma; and the name of the giant was Hope.

'Therefore,
this is the word of the Lord concerning the King of Assyria:
"He shall not enter this city,
nor shoot an arrow there.
He shall not advance against it with a shield,
nor cast up a siege ramp against it."'

The great voice rang louder and louder with triumph:

'"By the way on which he came, he shall go back:
this city he shall not enter.
This is the very word of the Lord.
I will shield this city to deliver it,
for my own sake and for the sake of my servant David."'

He stopped speaking, and in the deathly hush that followed we could hear the echo of his dying words reverberating around the eastern hills. Then a woman in the crowd began sobbing hysterically, and the spell was broken. Some cheered, some laughed, and many wept and embraced their neighbours. One of the men who turned and clasped me to his bosom looked like one of those who had hurled stones at me that morning. I suppose the procession of priests made their way back to the Palace to deliver their message, but no one heeded them any more. All I know is that suddenly Isaiah stood before me.

'Come, boy,' he said, and I followed. He swept down the steps and out through the Great Gate. The soldiers let us pass without a word, but swung the gates shut behind us. Down the slope we went, in full view of the Assyrian detachment on the opposite hillside, but they seemed to pay us little attention. Two of their horses stood riderless, and while the others looked on, one man knelt over the prostrate figure of another, as though he were wounded, or had been taken ill. As we crossed the brook, I saw another rider trotting northwards from the direction of their southern outpost. He paused by the first group, and then rode on as fast as the broken terrain would allow him.

Isaiah did not lead me towards the cluster of buildings where we had left Adad, but diagonally northwards, so that we eventually reached a sort of plateau overlooking the main Assyrian encampment. There were scenes of confused activity all over the area covered by the enemy forces. It seemed they were not planning on a long stay, for few tents had been erected. In one place, a column of smoke rose up, surrounded by what appeared to be ceremonial rings of priests, or perhaps the mashmashus Adad had spoken about, and watched by ranks of soldiers. Like the Judaeans, the Assyrians were evidently praying to their gods. Not all the soldiers, though; a number were lying out on the ground some distance away, and men passed among them carrying water pots, while away to the west, a detachment was busy with picks and spades.

'What are they digging?' I asked. It was not a sensible place for a siege ramp.

'Graves,' said Isaiah.

He strode on, passing to the north of the enemy camp and then swinging round to the south, to circle the city of Jerusalem beyond its western wall, across the road from Libnah and on towards the southern approaches. We had scarcely crossed the Libnah road when the sound of galloping horsemen made Isaiah pause and turn. He sat down on a rock, and I sank thankfully to the ground beside him. The horsemen passed by so close that I could hear the heaving of the horses' chests, and see the flecks of foam on their flanks.

'Messengers from Sennacherib?' I asked.

My grandfather nodded. 'The hand of the Lord is at work,' he said. He got up, and we continued on our relentless circuit. I was getting very tired; the sun had been on the point of setting behind Mount Moriah when I had followed my grandfather out of Jerusalem, and though we had gained another hour or so of daylight as we came round to the west-facing heights, night had now fallen. It was not dark, however, because a full moon shone out of a clear sky, and at last, in its cold light I saw the outline of the Mount of Olives come into view. We must have passed at least a dozen Assyrian outposts, several with one or two riderless horses, and three times urgent messengers had galloped past us, intent on their own affairs. Then, as we crossed the Hebron road, we met a complete detachment riding north, and leaving no one behind.

'What is happening?' I asked. 'Are they retreating?'

We were passing through the shattered remains of a cornfield; in the moonlight, Isaiah bent and picked up a few grains of unripe wheat, trampled into the ground before the harvest was due. 'This year,' he said, 'you will eat only the grain that has been scattered; next year only that which has sown itself on the wind; but the third year, my people will sow, and reap, and plant vineyards, and eat their fruit. Those that remain in Judah shall strike fresh root under ground, and yield fruit above ground. The zeal of the Lord of Hosts will perform this.'

I thought he was right about one thing; whether the Assyrians stayed, or left, months of hardship and famine lay ahead. But why, after months mounting this huge invasion of our land, and destroying all our fenced cities except one, should they pack up and go home without taking their prime objective, Jerusalem, the centre of church and government, the seat of kingship, the crowning glory of Sennacherib's conquests?

I tried to ask my grandfather this, but he was not really interested in the logic of mortals, and I was too hard put to it trying to keep up with his tireless strides to spare my breath for questions. At last, at long last, we came within sight of the old woman's hovel.

'Go in, now, and sleep,' he told me, and I went, like a harried fox to its earth. Where Isaiah went, I have no idea. I crept in by the half-open door, and, having found Adad by the gleam of the moon that filtered in through the narrow window, I flung myself down on the sleeping mat beside him, and knew no more.

Chapter 10

I slept until late in the morning, and woke to find myself alone in the room. I got up and went outside and saw the old woman baking meal cakes over a fire of twigs. She offered me some, hot and fresh, and a drink of goat's milk. I assumed her position as unofficial caretaker of the Prophet's bodily needs cast a mysterious kind of protective net over her, as she seemed troubled neither by foreign marauders, scavenging refugees nor the increasing numbers of men driven by desperation into banditry. She lived, with her goat and her meal cakes, unluxuriously, as she had always done.

'Where is Adad?' I asked casually, as I drained my bowl of milk.

'The Blind One? He has gone to the graves of his people.'

'What?' I stood aghast, my heart motionless, the blood draining from my face. After all we had endured together, while I slept, as easily as that. 'What happened? Why didn't I hear anything?'

'You were sleeping when the sick man came by. The Blind One said to me, "Tell the boy that I have gone to the graves of my people; he will know where to look for me." Then he left, with the sick man. The soldier could have stayed here, but he would not; he wanted to find his priest.'

'You mean, Adad went willingly? The Blind One is not dead?'

She shook her head. 'The Blind One has been touched

by the Holy Prophet; he has not the spirit of death. It was the sick man who will die.'

I was not concerned about the sick man, whoever he was, but I was not at all sure what was meant by Adad's message—except, that is, that he was neither dead nor, apparently, in danger. I felt the warm blood pulsing through me as the truth sank in. The old woman must have seen the relief in my face, for she smiled as she handed me a second bowl of milk, and commented, 'The Blind One is your friend.'

I nodded, and asked her where she thought Adad had gone. She pointed north-west towards the Assyrian camp, so as soon as I had finished the milk, I set off in that direction, wondering very much what I should find.

The camp site was deserted, apart from a few loose horses wandering about, and two distant figures, one of whom, as I drew nearer, I recognized as Adad, and by then I could distinguish a third man, lying on the ground. They were all grouped a little away from the main encampment area, in the place where I had seen the soldiers digging what Isaiah had told me were graves. I understood the meaning of Adad's message, and half-guessed at the kind of disaster that had overtaken the invaders, remembering the galloping messengers of the night.

The second man was evidently a priest celebrating the funeral rites for the dead, with Adad and the sick man as the only mourners. I could not see how either of the Assyrians could pose a danger to me, so I slipped quietly up to Adad, and said, 'It's Benjamin,' as usual. He nodded, and drawing me to one side, began to explain what had happened. The priest glanced at me, and Adad said, 'It is all right; he will not harm you,'—not to me, but to the priest, who returned to his incantations and burnt offerings.

It appeared that the messengers I had seen riding from Libnah had come with news that the great encampment around Lachish lay crippled from the ravages of fever, spreading like fire through the closely-packed tents.

Sennacherib, himself at Libnah, had sent notice of his latest victory back to the base camp, and this was the news his emissaries had brought back to him. Already the same disease was beginning to infect his advance troops, so he had then sent urgent riders to the Rabshakeh, instructing him to withdraw from Jerusalem. As I had seen last night, a number of the Rabshakeh's own men had brought the infection with them, the latest casualty being the sick man who, abandoned by his comrades, had stumbled, desperate for a drink of water, to the old woman's door, wanting only to rejoin his people. Adad had helped him back to the camp where the only living man to be found was a priest, who had courageously remained behind to perform the religious rites for those who had died. What would happen to *him* if he was taken by Hezekiah's men I did not like to think; probably he would be ceremonially hewn to pieces upon the Great Altar in front of the Temple. It could not be long before the King sent out reconnoitring parties, and soon all Jerusalem would know that the door of their cage had been left open, and their captors had fled.

As I stood watching the priest and Adad fulfilling their pious duties to the men who had died far from home, I experienced that same sense of unreality that had enclosed me like a bubble when I first came in sight of Jerusalem after the destruction of Lachish. Where did I belong? Not to the cult of Assur, the god of destruction in whose name the Assyrian hordes swept through one defenceless neighbour after another; but not to the Temple cult of my Uncle Shebna and his associates either, with their narrow loyalties and their comfortable hates. The magnanimity of my mother and the gentleness of my father mingled in my veins with enough of my grandfather's uncompromising yearning for truth to make me for ever dissatisfied with easy mob loyalties. It was not for nothing that I had been on the receiving end of the stones, down in the pit of the Pool of Siloam with Adad. Just as Shear-jashub and Isaiah had never, in their different ways, quite fitted into the world of the Temple and its pious priests and yet had never been able to tear themselves away, so it would be with me; always needing its assurances, never satisfied with its limitations.

I sighed, burdened by loneliness, and Adad laid his hand on my shoulder.

'This should be a time of triumph for you,' he said. 'There will be rejoicing in Jerusalem today.'

'Yes,' I said, 'yes.'

'After the priest has finished, I will ask him to intercede with the god of the sun, Shamash, for the sight of my eye.'

'And then?'

'You have a home and family, and a place in the world. Times will be hard, but your people will survive, and you will grow up to be a better priest than your uncles.'

'And you?'

'I will go with Hannah to Samaria. She has told me that is where she wants to go, once all this is over, to be with her own people. And that is where the Holy Man lives who can perform miracles of healing.'

'What about your priest, this one here?'

Adad's face clouded. 'I must ask him, too. I must ask everyone. I cannot stop seeking till I have the sight of my one eye back. Every man, every god; and the one who gives me back my sight, him I will worship.'

I said nothing. I could not blame Adad. I could not say to him, 'It may be the will of the All-Seeing that you remain blind,' just as Isaiah saw the Assyrian invasion as the will of God. My Uncle Shebna would tell him he was blinded for his sins, which meant, if you looked at it the other way, my Uncle Shebna must be sinless because he was fat and prosperous; Aunt Leah, too.

The priest's ceremonies had come to an end, no doubt much shortened owing to circumstances, and Adad was speaking to him urgently. The priest took Adad's face in his hands, and stared closely at the closed eyelids still stitched up by the Jewish physician. Then he went to pick up the bowl of water standing near the sick man, and paused to kneel down and examine him. He had fallen unconscious, his only sign of life being an uncontrollable shaking from time to time. The priest poured a little of the water on to his lips, but it just dribbled off down the side of his face. The priest shook his head, and turned back to Adad. He must have said something to him about me, because Adad turned and called out, 'Watch for men coming from the city.' I moved to a patch of high ground from where I could see the approaches to the Fish Gate, and also keep an eye on Adad and the priest.

The priest got Adad to kneel by a flat stone, and prostrate himself several times on the ground, while he made some kind of paste with the water, some dust, and various herbs or meal or bits of dried fruit he took from a pouch. It was all done with a great deal of intoning of prayers and gestures of supplication, but I noticed that the priest kept a wary eye on me, to see that I was watching the gate, and was not up to any treachery.

I could see a lot of activity around the Fish Gate, and it was obvious a reconnoitring party was being assembled.

'Is anyone coming?' called the priest.

'No,' I said. 'Not yet.' I said no more, for Adad's sake.

The prayers went on. The priest took a wisp of dry grass and set it on fire with a reflector of polished metal in the bright sunlight; he crumbled dust over it, and wiped Adad's eyes with the ash. The sick man suddenly sat up with a wild cry, and began gabbling in an unfamiliar language. He must have been from one of the outlying races Sennacherib had subdued, dying for a foreign king in a foreign country.

The movement of men around the gate detached itself, and turned into a compact body, marching purposefully towards the deserted Assyrian camp. I let them proceed for a while, until the various anointing processes were over, and the priest was intoning again. Then I called, 'They are coming!'

The priest, to do him justice, finished his prayer, and then ran up beside me.

'Yes,' he said. 'It is time for me to go. Can you catch me one of the horses?'

'What about the sick man?' I asked.

'I will see to him,' he said.

I caught the trailing reins of a horse quite easily; it looked a tired and underfed creature, and plodded after me towards the priest. He was kneeling by the sick man, muttering prayers. Then suddenly, he slipped his left hand gently over the man's staring eyes, and with his right, pulled a shining blade out of his robe and struck down, powerfully, into the man's heart. The man arched up in a quick writhing movement, and fell back with a gurgling sound, blood welling up from the wound. With a steady hand, the priest wiped the knife on the man's tunic before folding it away in his robes again. Then he raised his arms up to the skies in a final invocation to a god of whom I had not heard till then—Marduk ('He must have been a Babylonian,' Adad remarked to me later) and took the reins of the horse from me.

'It was best for him,' he said, seriously, and leapt on to the horse's back with the agility of a young cavalry officer, and galloped away to the west, just as the soldiers came panting up the last slope.

'Are all your priests like that?' I asked, thinking how I had mocked Adad's 'mashmashus'.

'No,' he said. 'I was lucky. Most would have done nothing for me without gifts.'

We had both lived so long together in a kind of refugee no man's land, that I do not believe it occurred to Adad any more than to me that he, too, stood in danger of falling prey to Judaean vengeance. Only now, with the purposeful soldiers breasting the hill, did the truth strike us.

Adad clutched me. 'Where can I hide?' he muttered.

'There is no time,' I answered. To try and run now would be disastrous. 'Just say nothing; pretend you are dumb.'

'But . . .'

'Ssh! They are here. Act shocked—out of your wits.'

The men slowed and looked all around as they reached the edge of the camp site. Then they advanced slowly, spreading out, noting the dead fires, the trampled ground, the fresh graves and the newly-dead man. The officer in charge beckoned to me, and I walked over to him, leading a passive Adad behind me.

'What has happened here? Why are you here?'

I told him I was Isaiah's grandson, and been put in charge of this blind refugee from Lachish, who was in my grandfather's care. While I slept, he had wandered off, and I had followed him and found him here. It was all true, so far as it went. Adad stood with slack jaw and hands hanging limply. 'He is not. . . .' I tapped my head.

The officer nodded. 'There was a horseman rode away.'

'It was one of their priests, stayed behind to bury their dead.'

'Could you not stop him? Drive the horses away?'

'He had a knife. He killed that man.'

He went over, and joined some of the soldiers who were examining the dead man. Others were uncovering the bodies that lay huddled in the shallow makeshift grave. Words like 'sickness', 'pestilence', 'the hand of the Lord' drifted across to us, but nobody paid us any further attention.

'Come,' I said to Adad. 'It is time I took you home.'

I dropped him off at the old woman's cottage, for it would have been madness to try and take him into Jerusalem.

By the time I got back into the city, rumours of every sort were swirling round like floodwater: Sennacherib was marching to Egypt, which was plotting with Ethiopia; he was hastening back to Assyria to quell a revolt headed by his sons; he was dead, and his whole host with him, eighty-five thousand smitten in a single night; Babylonia had declared war against Assyria, and the two giants were destined by Jehovah to destroy each other. Then there were wise men in corners, muttering that none of these things were true; they were all false information circulated by Assyrian spies to put us off our guard, and suddenly Sennacherib and his mighty army would sweep up on every side and march in through our unwatched gates, and hew us all to pieces in their hour of triumph. Someone even went so far as to declare that one of the spies was none other than a blind son of the Rabshakeh himself, who had infiltrated the city through the Siloam water course.

It was forty-eight hours before a single view of events came to be gradually accepted, and even then there were, and still are, variations. Some said it was the spreading sickness that persuaded Sennacherib to withdraw, and others that it was unrest at home. The more knowlegeable reckoned it to be a combination of the two, allied to the fact that Hezekiah had already heaped most of the treasures of the city upon the Assyrian invader in an attempt to buy him off, so there was little to be gained from sacking Jerusalem except the replenishment of his vast army of slaves, and prestige.

Uncle Shebna officiated over a splendid sacrificial thank-offering, with Hezekiah, glorious in jewelled robes, ceremonially cutting the throat of a choice bull-calf, surely the last to have escaped slaughter through the hungry days. Nothing, however, could hide the stripped Temple walls, and there was no free feasting for the vast and hungry population of refugees. Indeed, attendance at the thank-offering was noticeably thinner than at the penitential one, and it was said that people would come to God to save their skins, but not to thank him once their skin was safe, unless there was a chance of a good meal for their trouble. In fact, the once torpid city was stirring and restless. Many of the menfolk, or in some cases whole families, began slipping off back to their villages to see what could be salvaged from the land, and others from the bigger cities like Lachish and faraway Beersheba began the long trudge to their ruined homes. The citizens of Jerusalem were glad to see them go, but if they thought everything would soon return to normal, they were mistaken. For thousands of the old, and for destitute widows with young children, the only hope of life was to stand at the street corners with begging bowls. Mothers sold their daughters for the price of a bowl of lentils, and young boys waited hopelessly in the market place for someone to hire them. Even now, fifteen years later as I write this, Jerusalem is packed to the limit of those new walls Hezekiah threw up, and though people no longer starve to death in the streets, the old grand days of a close-knit prosperous community are gone for ever, or so it seems.

I, too, left the city as soon as the thank-offering was over. For me, at any rate, it offered a free meat meal, some of which I took out secretly to Adad.

'Tomorrow,' I said, watching him eat, 'I shall go with you to Samaria. You, and Hannah, and Joel and Rebecca.'

'You? You will?' His unforced delight warmed me. 'But why? Your home is here, with your mother.'

'My mother agrees I should go. Unless . . . *until* you get your sight back, you need me, and Hannah needs me too. There will be a lot of robbers, and maybe stragglers and deserters from the Assyrian army; or what if Hannah falls sick? You could all starve to death on the journey. I can forage for food, maybe get some work; and I can bring some money, and am less likely to be robbed.'

'Oh, I know, I know. But even for you, it is dangerous, and you are the eldest son; your place is at home.'

'No,' I said. 'Not yet. There are my uncles. You've seen them—well, heard them—and know what they're like. The other relations, the ones from outside Jerusalem, they will leave us, and go home. But Shebna and Joah and Leah—now that my father is dead—they intend to live in our house, and look after my mother and sisters. My mother doesn't like it, but she can see it is best for the others—my little brothers and my sisters. But not for me. I am too old, and not old enough. Do you understand?'

Adad laughed, that rare laughter of his that always surprised me. 'Then you will come back with a beard and a deep voice, and say, "Uncle Shebna, this is my house. You can go now."'

'Well,' I said, stroking my silk-smooth chin, 'maybe I can't stay away that long. But things will be easier in a year's time. There will be more food to go round, and all this will be past history. I suppose I *could* live with Uncle Shebna if I had to, but not with Aunt Leah. Not at the moment.'

I left Adad, and walked up the hill to try and find my grandfather, to bid him goodbye. No one had seen him since the night he had led me round Jerusalem; he had not come to join in the rejoicing at the Temple.

I found him in the clearing in the olive grove. He was leaning against one of the gnarled old stems, as still and sinewy and weathered as a buttress of the trunk itself. One arm lay outstretched along a branch, and his head drooped low on his chest. He was murmuring to himself quietly most of the time, but now and again he would lift up his head and let out an almost wordless howl of anguish, and when he did this, I saw his face was drenched in tears.

The noise of revelry, the shouting and trumpet blowing, echoed clearly across the Kidron, and I caught some of my grandfather's words about the people who had gone up on the housetops to rejoice that the oppressors were slain, but not with the sword; then he turned once more to the waterworks of which Hezekiah was so proud, and the new walls he had built from the stones of the houses of the poor.

'Ye also made a reservoir between two walls for the water of the pool,' he muttered, and then raised his voice to echo through the quiet trees, 'but ye looked not to the Maker of it all, or consider Him who fashioned it long ago.'

His voice dropped again, till I could scarcely hear him. 'On that day, the Lord, the Lord of Hosts, called for weeping and beating the breast, for shaving the head and putting on sackcloth; but instead there was joy and merry-making, slaughtering of cattle and killing of sheep, eating of meat and drinking of wine, as you thought, for tomorrow we die.'

Suddenly he stood up straight and, grasping me by the shoulders, stared down into my face, his eyes fierce and probing behind the tears; yet it was not me that he saw.

'The Lord of Hosts has revealed himself to me; in my hearing he swore: "Your wickedness shall never be purged until you die."' Then he gazed out over my head, intoning like a priest at the Temple sacrifice, 'This is the word of the Lord, the Lord of Hosts.' His hands dropped to his sides, and he fell into a trance-like silence.

I found I was shaking like an olive leaf, and cold all down my spine. It was not that I feared his words to be a curse laid personally on me, but that through his physical weight upon my shoulder the awesome power of the prophet had swept through me; I felt as though the forked lightning had laid hands upon me.

After a while, Isaiah, too, began to tremble, and droop like the old man that he was.

'Sit,' I said, and lowered him, unresisting, to the ground. Now his eyes were dull as pebbles, and he closed his lids wearily.

I sat down beside him, and asked why, when all Jerusalem had despaired, he alone had faith in their salvation; and now, when the city rang with rejoicing, did he alone despair? But he did not answer. I do not think he heard me.

After a while, he seemed to be dropping off to sleep. I touched him hesitantly and said, 'I have come to say goodbye; I am travelling up to Samaria, to the city of Samaria, with the Blind One. I will return at the next latter rains. Will you give me your blessing?'

He nodded absently, but did not open his eyes. However, when I lifted his hands and placed them on either side of my head, he murmured, as though from a great distance, 'The Lord bless and keep you, son of Shear-jashub.'

I went back and told the old woman about him; she just went on breaking small sticks for the fire, and said, 'He will be hungry when he returns; it is always so.'

Chapter 11

Fifteen years have passed since the day my father died and Adad came into my life, but writing about all the events of those days has brought back memories so sharp-edged as to demolish the passage of time. By contrast, my recollection of our journey north, with Hannah and the children, has become blurred, the various adventures and hardships telescoping into a single indistinguishable impression. We were often hungry, and often disheartened; robbed once, nearly murdered once; and, when Rebecca lay almost dying from dysentery and malnutrition, were reduced to sending Adad out into the streets of Shechem with the blind man's begging bowl.

Hannah had hoped to find some of her family left in the capital, Samaria, and here, too, she told Adad, lived the Holy Man who worked miracles of healing. The Assyrian priest, when he had anointed Adad's eye with a sacred mud, had told him not to remove the stitches put in by the Jewish doctor. 'When it is the will of Shamash that you should see, the thread will dissolve away, and you will see as far as the snows of Hermon.' I had never seen Mount Hermon myself, but I knew it stood like a great snow-capped sentinel at the northern tip of the old Kingdom of David. Beyond, lay the homelands of Assyria, Adad's people.

Now, all the northern part of the Kingdom of David already lay in Assyrian hands, ever since Sennacherib's father had taken Samaria over twenty years ago. It was a strange country to journey through, full of strangers, for

Sargon, the Assyrian conqueror, had transported twenty-seven thousand of the population to work as slaves in distant lands, and replaced them with natives of Babylonia and Syria, cut off from their homelands by the mountains to the north and the desert to the east. In general, it was the teachers and leaders who were the ones to be transported, and the poor and uneducated who were left, so that in Samaria there existed a curious sort of shapeless equality between the simple folk in their own familiar homeland, and the clever, rootless, enslaved peoples exiled there; the only rulers were the Assyrian army commanders, whose job of keeping order was made much easier by the total disruption of the society which they governed. There were no established patterns of behaviour to which the people could conform, no tribal allegiances to which they could adhere. The whole populace seemed to exist in a bubble of unreality such as I had experienced twice in my life, but for them it had become a way of life.

From Shechem we crept on to Samaria, a pale and grizzling Rebecca hunched limply on the faithful Bathsheba. Adad strode out the most strongly, fortified by the knowledge that it was he, with his begging bowl, who had saved the little group from disaster, and hopeful of finding the Holy Man who would restore his sight. For Hannah, the hopes of finding her family had grown dim; incessant cares and lack of food had worn her to little more than an envelope of skin covering gaunt bones, but still she plodded on, taking life as it came without complaint.

Then, as we entered Samaria Joel suddenly cried, 'Look!' and ran away through the crowd milling around the market place.

'Joel! Come back!' called Hannah, and I dodged between the street-sellers after him.

The potter, with his small neat head and slight figure, had his back to me, but I would have recognised him at once even without the sight of Joel's eyes shining at me over his shoulder.

I turned back to the others. 'It is Joash,' I said. 'He is over there, selling pots.'

That evening we ate well, and slept under a roof, or at least, started the night thus, an unaccustomed luxury; but the hot darkness soon pressed in on me, for it was now summer, and I crept up with my sleeping mat to lie out on the roof under the stars. I was joined by Adad, who also could not sleep. The moment of joy for Hannah had been followed by disappointment for Adad; the Holy Man had fled after some trouble with the Assyrian authorities, and was now rumoured to be living near Megiddo, Solomon's famous 'second city'.

'If he is still alive,' said an old fig-seller, who remembered Hannah as a small child, before the fall of Samaria. 'He was an old man then, and that was nearly ten years ago.'

Of Hannah's immediate relations, none, it seemed, remained. Her parents' generation had all died, or been killed, and her brothers deported. Her sister had married a Syrian and moved away, but it was possible there might be some cousins still in the area; the fig-seller did not know, and there was no one else to ask. Anyhow, it no longer mattered very much; Joash had set up a nice little business selling small perfume jars with the owners' names inscribed on them—he had neither the equipment nor the money to buy materials for the great water pots.

Joash would always be able to set up a nice little business—he was a natural survivor. The wonder was that we had ever given him up for dead, and when I came to think about it, I realized that Hannah never had. She had never mourned him for dead, or dressed as a widow, or spoken of him to the children as though he were dead. I do not believe she ever seriously considered he had been taken into slavery, and even if he had been, she probably knew he would find a useful little niche for himself. Her fear had been simply that she would never find him again.

'I thought, if I came here, and traded by the gateway, sooner or later you would come and find me,' he said, which made very good sense; and there was no doubt he was delighted to be reunited with his children, and content to let Hannah, as soon as she arrived, take over the preparation of the meal. I fancy, though, he would have been happy enough to go on working away at his pots, and in due course find another woman to care for his needs.

Adad and I stayed there for ten days, resting in the sultry noonday, and in the cool evenings going out to dig the red clay subsoil that Joash needed for his trade. Then we moved on, to the north. It was the month of the grape harvest, which was a good time to travel, as we could easily find work for both of us; even Adad could join in the treading of the grapes and take his place in teams carrying the baskets laden with fruit from the vineyards. The land was much more fertile than in the Judaean hills that I knew, and though the retreating Assyrian forces had pillaged some of the crops, we were well to the east of the route followed by the main army. Samaria, impoverished though it was by the loss of its leading men, and the heavy toll of tribute money exacted every year by the Assyrian overlord, at least had known peace for the last twenty years, and the further north we went, the greater the signs of prosperity. Another advantage was that in such a mixed community the fact that Adad was an Assyrian and I a Judaean aroused little comment. Most people were reticent about their origins, for everybody had been somebody's old enemy, and apart from the military overlords in their uniforms there was a general feeling that the only way to make the best of things was to live and let live. In fact, a new breed of children were growing up, the product of mixed marriages, who were simply Samaritans. I had heard my Aunt Leah speak of these children with disgust, and Uncle Shebna often preached long sermons holding up the Israelites of the Northern Kingdom as a fearful warning to us in Judah to hold fast to the purity of our religion, and not to be seduced into mingling with people who worshipped other gods.

Our journey to Megiddo, following a roundabout route in search of work, took us through the Vale of Jezreel, one of the most fertile districts in the whole of Palestine; and I was happy enough to dawdle along, enjoying my freedom and the simple days of hard manual labour, which offered such a change from my sheltered, priestly upbringing. Adad's background had taught him to regard such work as degrading, but his whole world had fallen about his ears that day outside the walls of Lachish, and the life he was painfully rebuilding for himself had begun from the stony base of total helplessness. He did not enjoy the labour in the sun, as I did, but he accepted it, and grew strong and self-reliant. One side of his face would always remain sightless, but the scar from the Captain's sword healed to a narrow white ridge across the sunburnt face. The new hot pink skin that grew to replace the old burnt tissue on the other side dulled to a purplish flush that faded and merged into his naturally dark skin; but the bright sun continued to give him headaches, and the stitches put in by the Jewish doctor began to fray and irritate, so he made himself a leather patch, which he wore all the time. When I suggested he should take it off when the sun had dimmed towards evening, he said there was no point. He did not seem to want to test his eyesight, preferring to wait for some magic revelation, and came more and more to pin his hopes on Hannah's Holy Man.

So we came to Megiddo. I marvelled at the great buildings, the Palace and stables, and even the Shrine that Solomon had built there; though it seemed strange to me that our great King should have wanted to encourage a centre of worship right away from the Holy City of Jerusalem, for all through my lifetime Hezekiah had been concerned with destroying the High Places in Judah, as breeding-grounds for corrupt religious practice. Megiddo, though, was beyond his jurisdiction, being in the divided Kingdom now under Assyrian rule; and the Assyrians did not seem too bothered about the religious beliefs of the peoples they conquered, so long as they could exact tribute and slave labour from them. Adad ran his hands along the walls, surprised at the precise workmanship which produced great slabs of rock fitting so close together that no mortar was needed, or very little, to seal the joints. I told him of the hordes of Phoenician craftsmen Solomon had employed, and he replied, 'I thought as much; you Jews are rotten builders.'

We had not come to Megiddo as sightseers, however, but our enquiries about the Holy Man produced blank faces. At last one old woman, with whom he had once lodged, told us he had moved to Nazareth, up in the hills on the far side of the Jezreel valley. So in due course we moved on again. Now the olive harvest was in full swing and the time for the Feast of the Tabernacles, when everybody in Jerusalem moved out into the country for one glorious week, camping and cooking in the open air, and gathering olives off the family trees—for most families had at least one tree out on the hillside—drinking the new wine of the just-completed grape harvest, singing and dancing, all in honour of Jehovah. Up here in Samaria, where the people and religions were so mixed, the religious aspect seemed to have disappeared under an orgy of merry-making, and I am sure my Uncle Shebna would have disapproved of a lot of the things that went on; but then he was never entirely at his ease with the happy-go-lucky celebrations back home.

The week ended, and so did the long hot summer. As everybody else packed their tents and went home, Adad and I climbed up towards Nazareth, perched on a ridge in the Galilean hills, and the rains broke in a spectacular thunderstorm over our heads. At first, the hot dry dust sang as it sucked up the hissing drops and the air smelt like paradise. Water began to form in little trickles, zigzagging like a column of ants, carrying a dusting of tawny soil on its back; then all turned to a sticky sludge through which we trudged with muddy feet; and by the time we came to Nazareth, floodwater, steaming and thick as gruel, bucked and tossed around our ankles.

Nazareth turned out to be a shabby little village, its inhabitants preoccupied with salvaging the relics of the harvest, and patching up leaky roofs. We only stayed there long enough to dry out some of our clothes, and learn that the Holy Man was now reputed to be living in Galilee, if he was still alive, somewhere near the shores of the lake, before continuing our journey. Now that all the harvesting was over we had no reason to delay, and pressed on, almost always in the rain, up and down the switchback hills of Galilee until we began the last steep descent to the shores of the lake. The day when I had my first sight of the Sea of Galilee was the first one since the thunderstorm that the gloomy grey skies broke up into patches of dappled bunchy clouds scudding across the blue; their shadows swept across the hills, luminously green after the rain, greener than I had ever seen my Judaean hills, and nestled among them, glittering like a diamond, lay the lake.

'Look!' I cried to Adad, forgetting.

We spent all winter by the Sea of Galilee but we never found the Holy Man. Instead, we found a fisherman living at the northern end, at a little village called Capernaum, who took us in to live with his family. We mended his nets—a task at which Adad was remarkably adept—and gathered wood for the fires which he used to smoke the fish which his brother and nephews carried into the hill country to sell; and we made ropes and patched his sails. On quiet days he took us out in his boat and taught us his craft; at first I was terrified of the fathomless waters below me, and watched apprehensively for the dark ruffle on the water under the western hills which warned of a rising wind, but as the weeks passed, I gained in confidence and began to take pride in my boat-handling skills. Adad never took to it, though he was willing to wade along the shoreline to work the nets. His real delight though, was in designing and building a new smoke-house for our fisherman. It worked much better than the ones the other fishermen used for preserving the deep-bellied scaly fish they brought ashore in their nets, and he began to pick up other jobs among the scattered villages round the lake side.

As the spring approached, I began to get restive, remembering my promise to return home by the latter rains, those sweet showers that, in a good year, fall on the newly sown corn and give it the necessary moisture to put down roots and grow and ripen through the waterless summer months. When there are no latter rains, people go hungry.

Adad, too, was restive. Seeing him at work on one of his building projects, I was reminded of Joash at his potter's wheel. The task soothed him, and while he shaped and shifted his stones he displayed the absorption of a craftsman who knows that what he is creating is good. But sometimes, when I came up and said, 'It is Benjamin,' he would turn to me with a ring of desperation in his voice, because he had laid down a tool and could not find it, or was driven to distraction by having to shift a heap of stones in order to feel each one over with his hands to discover its dimensions. Instead of growing accustomed to his dark world, it seemed to irk him more than ever; yet with that suppressed fury went an iron determination not to test the injured eye.

'I dare not,' he said, when I caught him in a reasonable enough mood to talk about it, for usually, if I touched on the subject, he retreated into an angry silence. 'I must wait for the miracle. That is what my priest said.'

'Perhaps he was wrong.'

'Don't say that, you must never say that.' He spoke with passion, and I fell silent. After a moment, he went on, trying to control the emotion that the tremor in his voice could not hide, 'Don't you see? What my gods began, your God must finish; then I will be free.'

'Free? Free to see?'

'That, of course. But free to be myself, in a new land. Free of the gods and people of my birth, who have rejected me.'

I did not entirely understand him. 'Supposing the Holy Man is dead?'

Adad did not answer at once, and when I glanced at him, I saw that his hands were clenched like a vice on the rock he was holding, and the burn scar glowed red against his whitened face. I put my hand out and touched him on the shoulder. 'There are other holy men who are healers,' I said.

'It has to be this one,' he muttered, and flung himself down on the ground and wept.

I wanted to tell him that he had woven himself into a cocoon of superstition so tight that he was suffocating himself; but how would that give him back his sight or set him free of the chains of his exile?

Next day, a sudden storm drove the fishermen and me to run ashore on a deserted spot on the eastern bank where a little spit of land offered some shelter. Juniper and terebinth trees covered the steep hillside above, and wattle hung in festoons of yellow arching branches along the foreshore. Having hauled up the boat, we pushed in among the bushes to find a little shelter for ourselves, and came upon a small hut, originally made of woven branches but now falling to pieces. It had obviously been inhabited within the last year, for a blackened fireplace was still discernible nearby, and some broken potsherds and a few old rags, including an ancient sleeping mat, lay around. The old fisherman found a comfortable bed of rock roses and juniper out of the wind, and stretched himself out to sleep. I pushed my way up through the undergrowth until I reached open hillside, only to retreat hastily into the shelter of the trees once I had felt the full force of the western gale.

Scrambling along just within the upper limit of the belt of trees, where the undergrowth was thin, I came upon a couple of boys, about my own age, tending a mixed flock of sheep and goats. They, like me, had come down off the open hill to find shelter. One of them was shaping himself a pipe out of a reed he must have gathered from the waterside, and I was prompted to ask if he knew anything about the deserted hut.

He told me that an old, old holy man had lived there for the past two years.

'Where has he gone?' I asked.

'Died,' said the younger boy, but his elder brother contradicted him.

'No,' he said. 'At least, he may have but we don't know.'

'He went to die,' insisted the younger.

I asked what he meant.

'He said he felt the approach of death, and he went to look upon Mount Hermon again before going to the everlasting darkness.'

'Mount Hermon?' I repeated, because I remembered the Assyrian priest's prophecy to Adad that when the time came he would see as far as to the snows of Hermon. 'Where would he do that?'

The boys seemed surprised that I had never seen Hermon, but in truth I had spent the whole winter down in the hollow of the lake, and the only time when I might have glimpsed those northern heights was on our journey from Nazareth, and most of that time had been spent under lowering clouds.

'If you climb these hills you will see Hermon,' they said, pointing up behind us, 'but he wanted to go to the Holy Mountain of Tabor.' The older boy pointed across the lake, where, from the level at which we stood, we could see in the distance a rounded hump rising above the nearer range of hills fringing Galilee's western shore. It lay well to the south of the route we had followed from Nazareth, but if we had not made that detour we might well have come right past Tabor on our journey from Megiddo, for all the time we had been gathering in the grape harvest in the vale of Jezreel, the big wooded lump of Mount Tabor stood upon our horizon. In our search for the Holy Man, we had travelled in a complete semi-circle around his final resting-place, and now we might be too late.

As I expected, as soon as I told Adad what I had learnt, he wanted to set forth at once, that very evening.

However, the kindly fisherman offered to take us by the boat the twelve miles or so down to the southern end of the lake next day, which, as it saved us the considerably longer walk round the shores, we gladly accepted. From there, where the lake pours out into the Jordan river, we turned west and climbed up into the hills.

We had about ten miles to go, mainly uphill, with a big climb at the end to the top of the mountain, and although we had embarked before dawn, the sun was getting high in the sky by the time we said goodbye to our friend and employer. Nevertheless, Adad was determined to complete the journey in one day, and kept urging me to take the quickest route and not to lose my sense of direction among the twisting valleys. All the time, he kept walking as fast as his quick-tapping stick would let him. It was almost a year since he had stumbled painfully up the road from Lachish to Hebron. He had learnt an amazing amount about moving around confidently in his darkened world in that time, but that only made it harder than ever for him to endure dependence on others for finding his way around in strange country.

The sun set behind the great hump of Tabor as we began to climb the western slope. At first we were able to follow a track alongside terraced vineyards, and then through a grove of carob trees, where irises and cyclamen glimmered in the dusk but the scarlet anemones showed only as blackish blobs against the pale stony soil. When this gave way to a tangled mess of spiny undergrowth under a canopy of forest trees, I suggested we should stop for the night and make for the top in the early dawn. But Adad, to whom the gathering gloom made no difference, insisted we should go on; so I struggled upwards, finding what pathways I could, with Adad gripping my tunic with one hand, and with the other holding his stick to try and shield his face from unseen branches.

'We don't even know that he will *be* at the top,' I objected. 'He could be anywhere—if he's here at all.'

'He will be where he can see Mount Hermon,' said

Adad. 'At the top, or near it, facing north.'

Adad was right. As, at last, we breasted the rounded summit and began to drop a little towards the north, we came into the glow of the sunset. We seemed to be in an upland meadow, full of flowers and set about with ancient olives.

Against a steep ridge stood an old stone building. It could have been used as a shepherds' shelter, but looked as though in days gone by it had formed part of some sort of fortification. I led Adad to the entrance, and stood gazing into the interior, fearfully.

'Is anyone there?' I called. There was no answer; a small breeze stirred in the olive trees.

'Holy Father, blessed of God, I have come to ask you for healing.' Adad's voice, husky with emotion, grated loudly on the silence. He put out his hand to feel the side of the open entrance, and a startled bird flew out into the dusk from a hole between the stones. At once some tiny unseen fledglings burst into shrill outcry, woken from cosy sleep by the sudden exposure to the chill night air.

'Nobody can be living here,' I said, peering in, and as my eyes grew accustomed to the gloom, I knew I was right. Nobody was living here; the dark eyes that seemed to stare at me from a white face in the shadowy corner were the empty sockets in a human skull.

'Come, come away; there's no one there,' I said, for I did not know how to tell Adad what I had seen, but his highly-keyed nerves had shared in the message of my eyes.

'He is there; he is dead,' he said, and he walked in through the open doorway, and felt for the dead man's bones.

I stayed outside, talking to an unheeding silence. 'We don't know it is the Holy Man. It could be anyone. There are heaps of other holy men. He probably wouldn't have been able to help, anyway.'

Not a sound came from Adad. After a while, I summoned up courage to go inside, and found that he had moved away to the far end of what was actually a large and rambling building and was leaning against the wall, his face pressed to the stones. I tried to persuade him to come out, but got no response. Back near the doorway, what had once looked dark now seemed like half-light to my accustomed eyes, and I could see how the main skeleton of the man still lay more or less in a natural position but the smaller bones were scattered around at random. Jackals, maybe, or vultures, not time, had reduced the decaying frame to these clean-picked relics.

In vain I tried to rouse Adad from his self-isolation; he responded no more to my words than if his skull were as empty as the dead man's. At last I left him and, wrapping myself in my cloak, I lay down in the angle between two ruined walls outside the entrance.

I had meant to keep watch, but sleep overcame me. It was restless sleep, with strange dreams of a deep coldness crawling over me like soldier ants, picking and picking at my flesh till my very bones lay as cold and naked to the winds as that poor skeleton. Then warmth fell upon me like clothing and I sank into dreamless slumber.

When I awoke, it was bright morning, and the sun dazzled me. Looking down, I found I was wrapped in two cloaks, my own, and Adad's.

Where was he? I threw them off and got up; not seeing him outside, I went to look in the building. Light now streamed in through every crack, and I could see at once he was not there. While I stood quietly listening, the mother bird flipped into her hole by the doorway, beak full of grubs, to be greeted by a chorus of shrill twitters.

Outside, I stared around, heart full of fear, yet strangely unwilling to shout. It was truly an enchanted place we had stumbled upon in the twilight; an enchanted place to die. The ground sloped gently under the ancient olives, carpeted with bright flowers. Now the scarlet of the anemones blazed in the sunlight, only outshone by the golden crown daisies that ran riot over the stone walls; bright pimpernel with crimson eye sprawled everywhere, and clumps of soft purple iris and pale cyclamen grew in the dappled shade beneath the olives. The gnarled and overgrown trees were alive with birds going about their business, and it was following the turquoise and golden flash of a bee-eater as it swooped down over the lower rim of this little paradise, that I suddenly saw Adad.

He was sitting quite still, on a rock, just where the level sward of the upland meadow fell away to a steep and rocky incline. From where I stood, it could have been a precipice and, fearful for his safety, I approached quietly, to avoid startling him. His well-trained ear must have heard me, though, for as I came near he said, without surprise, and without turning round, 'Come and sit by me, and look at the snows of Hermon.'

It was something in his voice, rather than his actual words, that got to me first. I actually did look out, just as he told me, over the rolling plain, and the green northern hills blending into the more distant blue of the Heights of Golan, to the snow-capped peaks of Mount Hermon, sparkling in the fresh morning light against the clear sapphire sky.

Then I turned to look at him. He had taken off the leather patch. From the oval of pale skin that reflected the exact outline of the patch, from between reddened lids, his dark eye shone clear. He looked back at me and laughed.

'You are not a bit as I imagined you,' he said. 'I hope you're the same person.' He put his left hand over his seeing eye, and traced the contours of my face with his right. 'Yes,' he said. 'It's the same Benjamin all right.'

'Can you really see, properly?' I said. 'Can you really see Mount Hermon?'

'Yes,' he said. 'Now I can. I've had a few hours' practice, while you slept.'

He had not slept. I do not know how long he had stood against the wall in silent despair, or at what point he had made the decision to face the truth; sight, or perpetual blindness. He had taken off the patch without knowing whether it was daylight or darkness, and had felt his way to the doorway, looked eastwards and seen the sky silvering over the outline of the hills of Gilead, beyond the Jordan valley. I can only guess at the quiet joy that welled up in him as the sun rose and flooded the land with light.

'When did you give me your cloak?' I asked.

'Oh, quite early. I heard you muttering and whimpering in your sleep and I was going to wake you up, and tell you. But it was too dark for me to be sure, and when I felt how cold you were, I just covered you up and left you in peace.' He paused a moment, and then added, 'I have been praying for you, to my God and your God.'

'For me?' I said, startled.

'Yes, because I have got what I wanted, but you have not.'

'What do I want?'

He shook his head. 'I don't know. It is, I think, something you will never get.'

'That's nice.'

'I am serious.' He turned and stared at me with that disconcerting seeing eye. 'You must let me say this, because there are some things one can see better when blind—some truths, I mean. I think, now I have my sight back, I will only see flowers, and hills and houses, and not the things beyond, so now I must tell what I have seen, before I forget.'

'All right,' I said. 'Tell me. What is the thing that I will never get?'

'Truth? Wisdom?' It was a question, not an answer. 'God?'

'All men seek God.'

'No. You are wrong. Very few men seek God. Lots of men seek to *please* their gods. They don't really want to know *about* them. They just want things from them—long life, beautiful and faithful wives, many sons, many cattle, much gold. So they busy themselves doing the things their priests tell them will please the gods; sacrificing, killing, destroying; all right, helping widows and orphans too, but it's all part of the same game: obey the rules, do as you're told, and the gods will give you what you want. But you are different. You ask questions.'

'I don't think I do.' Whenever we had talked about religion, it was usually Adad who started it.

'Not in words. But the rules aren't good rules for you. You have something inside you stronger than rules. Why did you rescue me after Lachish, and again by the Siloam Pool? Why did you stand up against your Uncle Shebna? Why did you choose to leave your home and wander the countryside with the enemy of your people?'

'I don't know. I've never really thought about it. It just seemed the right thing to do at the time.'

Adad laughed. 'Like putting on my uniform and walking straight into the heart of the Assyrian army.'

'I was curious.'

'Curious. Independent. A seeker after truth. Those are the qualities an officer looks for in the men he sends out ahead of his troops, to spy out the land.'

I remember feeling warm and proud. I had not thought of myself like that, but now that Adad had painted the picture of some sort of spiritual leader, I quite fancied the part. After all, Isaiah was my grandfather. 'It sounds quite a good description of what a priest ought to be,' I said. 'I should like to think I could be that sort of priest.'

'Yes,' said Adad. 'Yes. That is why I was praying for you. Remember what can happen to people who go out ahead to spy out the land and find themselves alone among enemies.'

The gravity in his voice, and the memory of those impaled corpses before the walls of Lachish sobered me. Yet I could not really understand what he was talking about, and it seemed a strange mood to have fallen upon him at this joyful moment.

'Why are you trying to tell me this, now?' I asked.

He stood up. 'Because very ordinary men can be seers when they become blind, but as soon as they get their sight back, they become ordinary men again, who can only see things in front of their faces. Who wants more, when the world is such a beautiful place?'

'What will you do now?'

'I shall go back to Hannah and Joash, and then I shall go to Lachish.'

'To *Lachish*? Why?'

'To build houses for people to live in.'

I sat and stared out over the green hills, full of strange thoughts. Adad was right; I would go back to my father's house, because that was what was expected of me. What would I do, though, when I got there? Learn to be a young priest under the tutelage of my uncles? That meant learning how to slaughter a lamb or a calf in such a way that the blood sprayed on the altar stones without soiling the celebrant's fine white robes; learning the details of each ritual for every occasion that may befall a man between birth and death; learning how to whisper the right rumour at the appropriate time to cast a shadow of doubt about the worthiness of a rival for the next step up the priestly ladder; and especially, learning to the last featherweight exactly what proportion of each poor man's offering could legally be deducted for the priest's share.

There was another way, the way of Isaiah, but that was a way no man could choose; for that, he had to be chosen; and, being chosen, to let go of the normal chains of human intelligence and allow the divine revelations to flow freely; to be a little mad. A shiver of fear passed through me as I wondered whether, if that should ever happen to me, I would have the courage to submit. But somehow, I did not think that it ever would.

I remembered the strange thoughts that had come to me in the deserted Assyrian camp on the morning of Jerusalem's deliverance. If, indeed, as Adad said, my destiny was to search for the unsearchable mystery, I could never abandon the Temple and all it stood for, as Adad had abandoned his native land; for somewhere buried deep in its sacrificial cults lay the thing for which I was seeking; but if I stayed inside the system, I saw clearly at that moment, it would be to do battle against the Shebnas and the Eliakims alike. Adad could look forward to building himself a new home in every sense of the word; it was I who would always be an exile in my own land.

Adad suddenly broke into my sombre thoughts by saying, 'Do you see that track winding down past the big cedar tree?'

'No,' I said.

'There, halfway down the hill.'

'Oh, yes.'

'I'll race you to it.'

I looked at him blankly for a moment, and he laughed and put his arm round my shoulders. 'Cheer up,' he said. 'You don't have to lose. You might win.'

'The race?'

'Who cares about the race? I meant whatever you were thinking about, oh sighted one among the blind.'

'Perhaps that's as lonely as being blind among the sighted.'

Adad said, 'That's not as lonely as you think at first it's going to be. You may not have many friends, but at least you know who they are. When you get fed up with your Uncle Shebna, just come and visit the One-Eyed Builder of Lachish.'

I laughed, forgetting my mood of foreboding. 'What about this race, then? You'll have to give me a start. You've got longer legs.'

'Wait. There's something I've got to do first. And I'm hungry. What have we got left to eat?'

I produced some dry crumbled bread and a few pieces of smoked fish from the bag. Adad meanwhile heaped up a little pile of dead leaves on a flat stone and taking out his bright burning mirror, directed the spotlight of sunshine on to them. That was how we had made our fire all through last summer, but under the grey skies of winter we had depended on the fisherman's constantly tended hearth. This was the first time since the rains that we had used the mirror, and the leaves steamed sullenly.

'You keep trying,' said Adad. 'I've got to fetch the sacrifice.'

While I persevered, I wondered what he meant. Then, as the leaves reluctantly started to curl and smoulder, he returned with his eye-patch and tapping stick and some of the tatters from the Holy Man's clothing. He broke the stick in small pieces, and laid them tent-shaped on the crackling leaves, and soon we had a little fire burning palely in the bright morning light.

Adad fed the flames carefully with strips of rag and laid the leather patch on top, together with some of the bread and dried fish. I waited for him to begin his sacrificial prayers. He looked across at me through the eddying smoke, and grinned.

'To the God of Benjamin, and the God of Adad, to the God of Heaven and Earth, to the Unknowable One, I make this thank-offering,' he intoned, and I repeated the words after him. Then we sat down and shared the rest of the bread and fish between us.

'Now,' said Adad, when we had finished our meal, and scattered the ashes of our sacrifice over the bones of the Holy Man, and collected up our belongings, 'I'll race you to that tree!'

Epilogue

It was Adad who suggested I should try and record that eventful year when our boyhood was caught up in the drama of history. I am glad he did, although when I started to write two months ago, we both thought of it as no more than an occupation to while away the long days of hiding; but in the writing of these scrolls, something has happened; I have become aware of the way in which I am to be led by the hand of the Lord. I came here, to the house of Adad, the One-Eyed Builder of Lachish as all the people call him, when my world was crumbling about me more terribly than ever it did in the days of Sennacherib's invasion, because this time it has crumbled from within; we have betrayed ourselves, and betrayed Jehovah. I came here full of despair, but now I see a little hope, just as my father saw a little hope in these very walls which I look out upon from my window.

It is strange how, in foreseeing the future, one can often be right about the main drift of events and yet wrong about every detail. I returned home anticipating a long and difficult training under my Uncle Shebna, but I need not have worried on that score. Only a year after my return, Eliakim, who had the ear of the King, grew tired of his rival, and persuaded Hezekiah to choose Shebna as an emissary to Assyria with the promised tribute. I never discovered what links Eliakim had with those in power in Assyria, but poor Shebna never returned. Uncle Joah kept very quiet after that, and gradually all the important posts were filled with Eliakim's relations. By the end, Joah was little more than a doorkeeper.

My own position was pretty precarious, but I had the advantage of Isaiah as grandfather, and Hezekiah as protector, for he never forgot my small part in the siege of Jerusalem. I have pursued a quiet, scholarly course, collecting and recording the words of the prophets, and particularly those of Isaiah, and teaching the young students, Joel among them, and keeping well away from the power game. Joash soon had a thriving business going again back in Lachish, and, watching Rebecca growing up gentle and beautiful, it was in my mind to persuade my family that she would not be an unfit bride for me, even though she came only from a workman's family. But when I was preparing to go down to Lachish to make my proposal, I received a letter from Adad, asking me to officiate at his marriage to the daughter of Joash the Potter, and his wife Hannah.

I performed all the due sacrifices, and gave them my blessing, and if afterwards I joined in the singing and dancing and revelry with a sad heart, I tried not to let it show. In view of what has happened since, I suppose it was just as well that things turned out that way.

During these last few years, as the ageing Hezekiah grew more feeble, people began to talk in corners about his chosen successor, Manasseh. We saw little of him either at the Temple ceremonies or in the councils of state, though, if rumour spoke true, he was quite a familiar figure in that part of the city where painted women sat beckoning at their windows. There was talk, too, of drunken parties turning night into day within the Palace precincts whenever Manasseh was at home, but much of the time he was travelling abroad, to Phoenicia and Philistia, and south to Egypt, and latterly, more and more frequently, to Assyria. 'Keeping on the right side of our overlords', as Eliakim called it. I did not like the phrase, because we had never been conquered by the Assyrians, as Samaria had been, and though it is true we had to pay an annual levy in order to preserve our freedom, I did not see why we should pretend we liked them for it.

Eliakim always posed as a close friend of Manasseh, and was at pains to gloss over his shortcomings, and present him as an able and responsible young man. I do believe, with hindsight, that if Eliakim had not so consistently upheld Manasseh's right to inherit, Hezekiah might well have changed his mind about the succession, because he must have seen that he was not the man to carry on Hezekiah's own tradition of religious reform. But if Eliakim thought that he was ensuring for himself a position of power under the new King, he was in for a rude awakening.

The old King was scarcely laid to rest before a reign of terror began.

At first, we in the Temple did not realize what was happening. All we knew was that Manasseh never took part in the rituals because he was always visiting other towns around Judah. 'Getting to know the people,' Eliakim said, but it was young Joel who brought news of what was really happening. Manasseh had been in Lachish, he said, setting up the old 'High Place' which Hezekiah had dismantled, and practising all kinds of pagan rites; setting up idols and worshipping them, and calling his rabble of young men 'priests', and carrying away young girls to act as so-called 'priestesses'. It was not safe for women like Rebecca to be seen on the streets, and the tradesmen went in fear of having their gold and money impounded to pay for Manasseh's luxurious parties. It had been the same in Beersheba before that, Joel said.

While the priests in Jerusalem were mulling over this news, and Eliakim was finding himself in the agonizing position of having his two feet on either side of an ever-widening rift, Manasseh arrived back in Jerusalem and marched straight into the Temple with his gang of young men, bearing images of the bull-god Baal, and the she-goddess Ashterah, the very symbols of the cults Hezekiah had been so concerned to stamp out, and set them up in the holy Temple itself.

Now my difficulty, as Adad pointed out all those years ago, is that I'm better at asking questions than finding answers, whereas most of the priests are better at giving answers than asking questions, and one answer they all knew by heart was that Baal-worship was wicked, and forbidden utterly by Jehovah. It was one point on which they were at one with my grandfather. I, who had lived for a year with Adad and his Assyrian gods, have this feeling that men who worship truly have the same god at heart, whatever name they gave him—or even her, though I may say this idea of there being a god and a wife-goddess seemed a bit like inventing gods in the image of man, rather than worshipping a Supreme Creator, neither male nor female. All the same, when the whole school of priests began to scream with rage about the desecration of the Temple, I went home to think, and to talk with Isaiah. My grandfather was now a very old man, and at last had been driven from his beloved hills to end his days living quietly in the house of his daughter-in-law, where I, too, still lived. As a result, I was not in the Temple precincts when Manasseh's young men drew their swords and killed every priest in the place, Eliakim included.

The slaughter stunned Jerusalem. During the ensuing days, while Manasseh's men worked themselves up into a riotous frenzy in the hysterical drinking and sacrificing that followed the killings, I moved quietly from house to house, telling my students to disperse to their homes or to relatives in the country, and wait for me to contact them when the time was right. Yet what was I to do? I felt guilt and shame that I had not shared in the fate of men who, whatever their failings, had died in the service of the God whom I, too, served; but deliberately to court death, now, would be pointless.

There was, however, one thing to be done. I gathered up all the scrolls on which my students and I had been working, containing the records of the prophecies of Isaiah and the other prophets, packed them in panniers and rode down to Lachish. There I handed them over to Hannah, who stowed them safely in a row of pottery jars at the back of Joash's storehouse. They would be safe and dry there until the troubled times were over.

When I got back to Jerusalem, I was met by my mother in tears. Manasseh, in a drunken speech at the end of a massive feast he had thrown in an attempt to gain popularity, had said that, to show how much love he felt for his countrymen, he would ensure a bumper harvest for them by sacrificing to the fertility god, Baal, his very own son.

I stared at her, aghast, remembering the horror with which my father had spoken of King Ahaz, years back, doing just that. Had we learnt nothing? Were we to be dragged back to an age of barbarism? The God we worship, my father had said that day, is not the God of killing, but of saving. I knew then that while I had gone home to search my conscience, the day Manasseh had set up his idol in the Temple, it was the priests in their blind obedience who had known the true God from the false.

'Has he done it?' I asked.

She nodded. 'Yes, and that's not all. Your grandfather, when he heard of the King's boast, rose up, and left the house, and went and stood upon the top step of the Altar. He stretched out his hand, and forbade Manasseh to do this wickedness; and Manasseh took his sword, and slew him with his own hand, upon the High Altar.'

I took her hand, and led her indoors. 'Afterwards, they came here, looking for the records of his prophecies, to destroy them.' She straightened herself, and looked at me with a defiant smile. 'I would not let them in,' she said. 'When I saw them coming, I sent Abraham indoors and came to the gate myself, and told them what I thought of them.' There was a dark bruise on her cheekbone and her lip was cut and swollen. I sat down and drew her head on to my breast, and stroked her hair, just as she had done so often for me when I came crying to her as a child.

'An old man,' she said. 'The greatest in the nation. The glory of Judah, hacked to death like a jackal. And that little child. The old King's own grandson, whom he used to watch at play from his sickbed.'

Still I said nothing, but stroked the grey hair and knew the meaning of despair.

'I wish I had been here,' I said at last. I felt like the blemished lamb in the flock, always rejected for sacrifice as unworthy of Jehovah.

'I am glad you were not,' she said, looking sharply up at me. 'Who else is left for me in my old age, and to preserve the old teaching?' She got up and began to busy herself, as ever, bringing me warm water to wash, and preparing a meal. 'You must not stay, even for this night. It is not safe.'

'What about you? I cannot leave you here alone.'

'I have Abraham, and the other servants. Manasseh's men will not harm me. I am no threat to them.'

'I would rather take you away with me into the country.'

'What should I do there? This is my home, and all the friends I have left are here.'

She would not go. She lives in the old house still, remembering the past, enlivened sometimes by visits from my married sisters, bringing their children to see her. My two younger brothers are safe in Egypt, where they had gone as students before all this happened. One has married an Egyptian wife, the other is betrothed to the daughter of a Judaean family which had fled there. My mother wanted me to join them, and I have thought about it. There is quite a colony of the Jewish intelligentsia living in Alexandria, and I could find a job there easily enough, as a teacher and preacher. In the drear winter months that I have spent since then, writing and praying in Adad's back room, I have many times resolved to pack up and go as soon as spring returns, when the ways are passable and full of travellers so that I could make my journey unnoticed by Manasseh's men. There is no doubt that they are looking for me, and would destroy me if they could. Of the priests who escaped death on that first day of blood, some have been killed since, and many have thrown in their lot with the new regime. A few of the young ones, the idealists and the students whom I used to teach, are, I believe, in hiding like me, and waiting—waiting for me.

Since writing this story, I keep hearing the voice of my grandfather. 'The daughter of Zion is left as a cottage in a vineyard, as a shed in a garden of cucumbers, as a besieged city. Except the Lord of Hosts had left us a very small remnant, we should have been as Sodom and Gomorrah.' I had been to Gomorrah since then—what was left of it: a pile of dead ruins in a dead landscape, way down at the foot of the Dead Sea.

I told Adad and Rebecca yesterday that I intend to leave them as soon as the rains cease. Adad promised me two pack-animals, and Rebecca went to prepare food for a long journey.

'There is no need,' I told them. 'I am only going to Gath, and then to Libnah, and then, maybe up to Bethlehem, and Hebron, and Beersheba. I am not going to leave the country.'

Adad said, 'You will be killed.'

'Very likely. But until that happens, I can still teach the things that I believe in, around the villages and in the vineyards, on the threshing-floors and in the olive orchards. I shall not need a donkey, nor provisions; I shall not wear my priestly vestments. It may be many years before Manasseh notices a poor foot-traveller who wanders about his country from village to village. Besides, I believe there are many others who will follow my example. I shall go and visit them, each one separately, alone in their homes, in the next few weeks, and tell them what I intend to do.'

'Joel?' asked Rebecca.

'I spoke to him yesterday. He says he will come. There is one other thing I must ask you.'

'You know we are always your friends,' said Adad.

'The scrolls. You know where they are hidden. If I should be killed, and the time comes for Joash and

Hannah to be gathered to their forefathers, will you take them and keep them safe?'

'Of course. And when our time comes, they shall be handed into the safe-keeping of young Benjamin here,' said Adad, gathering up his two-year-old son, my namesake.

'Manasseh can't reign *that* long, I hope,' I said, and quoted from my grandfather's writings. 'Behold, a king shall reign in righteousness, and princes shall rule in judgement.'

'Don't wait for the kings and princes,' said Joel, who had come quietly in. He had never lost his childish excitability, and now his eyes were alight with fervour for this new challenge. 'Remember the next bit: "A man shall be as a hiding-place from the wind and as a covert from the tempest; as rivers of water in a dry place, as the shadow of a great rock in a weary land."'

. . . .

Overnight, the skies have cleared, and now the sun shines golden on the new Lachish walls. It is a good day to begin a journey which may last a week or a lifetime.

F Morgan, Alison
MOR
　　　The eyes of the
　　　blind

$13.95

17576

	DATE	

AKIBA HEBREW ACADY LIBY
223 NO HIGHLAND AVE
MERION, PA

12/26/90   13.95

625244   12907

© THE BAKER & TAYLOR CO.